The
Focus of the
Lord's Recovery

The Holy Word for Morning Revival

Witness Lee

Living Stream Ministry
Anaheim, CA • www.lsm.org

First Edition, December 2011.

ISBN 978-0-7363-4966-6

Published by

Living Stream Ministry
2431 W. La Palma Ave., Anaheim, CA 92801 U.S.A.
P. O. Box 2121, Anaheim, CA 92814 U.S.A.

Printed in the United States of America

11 12 13 14 / 6 5 4 3 2 1

Contents

Preface

1. This book is intended as an aid to believers in developing a daily time of morning revival with the Lord in His word. At the same time, it provides a limited review of the Thanksgiving weekend conference held in San Jose, California, November 24-27, 2011. The subject of the conference was "The Focus of the Lord's Recovery." Through intimate contact with the Lord in His word, the believers can be constituted with life and truth and thereby equipped to prophesy in the meetings of the church unto the building up of the Body of Christ.

2. The content of this book is taken primarily from the conference message outlines, the text and footnotes of the Recovery Version of the Bible, selections from the writings of Witness Lee and Watchman Nee, and *Hymns,* all of which are published by Living Stream Ministry.

3. The book is divided into weeks. One conference message is covered per week. Each week presents first the message outline, followed by six daily portions, a hymn, and then some space for writing. The message outline has been divided into days, corresponding to the six daily portions. Each daily portion covers certain points and begins with a section entitled "Morning Nourishment." This section contains selected verses and a short reading that can provide rich spiritual nourishment through intimate fellowship with the Lord. The "Morning Nourishment" is followed by a section entitled "Today's Reading," a longer portion of ministry related to the day's main points. Each day's portion concludes with a short list of references for further reading and some space for the saints to make notes concerning their spiritual inspiration, enlightenment, and enjoyment to serve as a reminder of what they have received of the Lord that day.

4. The space provided at the end of each week is for composing a short prophecy. This prophecy can be composed by considering all of our daily notes, the "harvest" of our inspirations during the week, and preparing a main point

with some sub-points to be spoken in the church meetings for the organic building up of the Body of Christ.

5. Following the last week in this volume, we have provided reading schedules for both the Old and New Testaments in the Recovery Version with footnotes. These schedules are arranged so that one can read through both the Old and New Testaments of the Recovery Version with footnotes in two years.

6. As a practical aid to the saints' feeding on the Word throughout the day, we have provided verse cards at the end of the volume, which correspond to each day's scripture reading. These may be removed and carried along as a source of spiritual enlightenment and nourishment in the saints' daily lives.

7. The conference message outlines were compiled by Living Stream Ministry from the writings of Witness Lee and Watchman Nee. The outlines, footnotes, and references in the Recovery Version of the Bible are by Witness Lee. All of the other references cited in this publication are from the ministry of Witness Lee and Watchman Nee, which is published by Living Stream Ministry.

Thanksgiving Weekend Conference
(November 24-27, 2011)

General Subject:

The Focus of the Lord's Recovery

Banners:

The unique focus of the Lord's recovery
is the testimony of the Triune God—
the corporate expression of the Triune God,
the testimony of Jesus.

Romans 8 is the focus of the entire Bible
and the center of the universe.

The focus of God's economy is the mingled spirit—
the divine Spirit mingled with the human spirit—
a spirit that is both the Spirit of the Lord
and our spirit.

We need to live in the focus of the Lord's recovery
as inoculators and ministers of the new covenant.

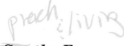

The Need to See the Focus
of the Lord's Recovery

Scripture Reading: Eph. 3:16-17a, 19b; Rev. 1:2, 9, 12, 20; 2:5; 1 Tim. 3:9, 15-16

Day 1   **I. We need to have a vision of the Lord's recovery—a vision that revolutionizes us, governs us, controls us, directs us, preserves us, keeps us in the genuine oneness, and gives us the boldness to go on (Prov. 29:18a; Acts 26:19):**

A. If we have the vision of the Lord's recovery, we are directed toward God's goal, and our living is governed according to God's economy (1 Tim. 1:4).

B. If we do not have a clear and strong vision of what is on the Lord's heart concerning His recovery, we are not in the recovery intrinsically, and we are doing things in vain (cf. Rom. 2:28-29; 1 Cor. 15:2, 14, 58; 1 Thes. 3:5).

II. The Lord's recovery is unique in everything (Eph. 4:4-6):

A. In the recovery we have the unique God, the unique plan, the unique economy, the unique work, the unique way, the unique ministry, the unique focus, and the unique goal (1 Cor. 8:6; Eph. 1:4-5, 9-14; 3:9-11; 4:12-13, 16).

Day 2   B. The Lord's recovery is the recovery of the unique plan, the unique economy, the unique way, the unique work, and the unique focus by the unique ministry (Rom. 8:28-29; 1 Tim. 1:4; 1 Cor. 15:58; 16:10; 2 Cor. 3:8; 4:1; 5:18).

III. The unique focus of the Lord's recovery is the testimony of the Triune God—the corporate expression of the Triune God; this focus is the testimony of Jesus (Eph. 3:16-17a, 19b; 1 Tim. 3:9, 15-16; Rev. 1:9, 12, 20):

A. God's original intention was that man would receive His life and nature and thereby become His expression; the Lord's recovery is to recover the corporate expression of God (Gen. 1:26; 2:7-9; Col. 1:15; 2 Cor. 3:18; Col. 3:10).

 B. As the corporate expression of the Triune God, the church is the fullness of God (Eph. 1:22-23; 3:19b):

  1. The highest definition of the church is that the church is the fullness of God, the corporate expression of God (v. 19b).

Day 3

  2. In Ephesians 3:16-17a and 19b Paul prayed that the Triune God in Christ would make His home in our hearts so that our inner being would be filled unto the overflowing of the Triune God for the corporate expression of the Triune God; this is what God wants to recover today.

  3. As the corporate expression of the Triune God, the church—the Body of Christ—is a four-in-one organic entity—the Father, the Son, the Spirit, and the Body mingled together as one (4:4-6).

 C. The four-in-one organic entity in Ephesians 4:4-6 corresponds to the golden lampstands, the testimony of Jesus, in Revelation 1:9, 12, and 20; the churches as the golden lampstands bear the testimony of Jesus:

Day 4

  1. The testimony of Jesus is an all-inclusive expression (vv. 2, 9):

   a. *The testimony of Jesus* is the testimony of the Son coming with the Father and by the Spirit to live on earth, to die on the cross to clear up the universe, to release the divine life, and to resurrect from the dead to become a life-giving Spirit, who comes as the Son with the Father compounded with divinity, humanity, human living, crucifixion, and resurrection (John 1:14; 14:17-18, 20; 1 Cor. 15:45b).

   b. Such a compound testimony is the testimony of Jesus, and this testimony has a symbol—the golden lampstand (Rev. 1:2, 9, 12, 20).

Day 5

2. As the testimony of Jesus, the golden lampstand is the embodiment and expression of the Triune God (v. 12):

   a. In the golden lampstand there are ~~three~~ 3 main factors: T. G

      (1) The entire lampstand is gold; it is not only golden but gold itself, signifying God the Father's divine nature (2 Pet. 1:4).

      (2) The gold is in a definite form and a purposeful shape, signifying the Son, Christ, as the embodiment of the Godhead, the embodiment of the Father's nature (Col. 2:9; 1:15).

      (3) The seven lamps shining for God's expression are the seven Spirits of God (Rev. 1:4; 3:1; 4:5; 5:6).

Day 6

   b. In the lampstand we see the Father, the Son, and the Spirit; thus, the golden lampstand is the embodiment and expression of the Triune God.

   c. This is the church as the testimony of Jesus, the testimony of the Triune God, the expression of the Triune God (1:12, 20; 2:1, 5).

   d. In the church as the golden lampstand we have the Father's nature, the Son's embodiment, and the Spirit's expression; this should be the essence of the church's shining (Matt. 5:14-16; Eph. 5:8; Phil. 2:15-16):

      (1) The light that the church shines forth—the testimony that shines out from the church—must be the Triune God (Eph. 3:16-17a).

      (2) In everything we do in the church life and in our daily life, we must bear a clear, evident, strong testimony of a golden lampstand constituted with the Father's nature, the Son's embodiment, and the Spirit's expression (Rev. 1:20).

D. To bear such a testimony is to hold the mystery of the faith (1 Tim. 3:9):

now

1. The faith is the content of God's New Testament economy, in which we believe (Eph. 4:13; Titus 1:1, 4; Jude 3).

2. In using the word *mystery,* Paul refers to Christ as the mystery of God and to the church as the mystery of Christ (Col. 2:2; Eph. 3:4-6).

3. According to the context of 1 Timothy 3:9, the mystery of the faith should include the church, because the church is constituted with God in Christ and with Christ as the life-giving Spirit; this corresponds to the constitution of the lampstand (Rev. 1:12, 20):

   a. As the lampstand is constituted with the Father, the Son, and the Spirit, so the church also is constituted with the Divine Trinity (Eph. 4:4-6).

   b. The church is a living organism constituted with the living God in His Divine Trinity to be the corporate manifestation of God; this is not only the church but also the church life, the church's living (1 Tim. 3:15-16).

4. Thus, the church is a golden lampstand shining forth the corporate expression of the Triune God; this is the focus of the Lord's recovery—the testimony of the Triune God (Rev. 1:2, 9, 12, 20).

Morning Nourishment

Prov. **Where there is no vision, the people cast off**
29:18 **restraint...**
Acts **Therefore, King Agrippa, I was not disobedient to**
26:19 **the heavenly vision.**
Eph. **One Body and one Spirit, even as also you were**
4:4-6 **called in one hope of your calling; one Lord, one**
faith, one baptism; one God and Father of all, who
is over all and through all and in all.

What is God's ultimate move to carry out His intention? God wants us to have Christ as life to us, flowing in us, saturating and permeating us, transforming us, conforming us, and making us fit to be built up into His Body for His expression. Today...this is what our God is after. Here is where our focus also should be. (*The World Situation and God's Move*, p. 35)

Today's Reading

Under God's sovereignty the gospel has been preached to every corner of the earth. The Bible prophesied this would happen, and it has. The Bible has been taught in every country. And God did gain some proper meetings even a hundred fifty years ago. Even though God has gained this much, however, He has never gained the central line of His purpose, that is, Christ as the mystery of God and the church as the mystery of Christ. This church as the mystery of Christ must be the Body,...the new man,...the lampstand, [and] the bride.

We must look to the Lord to show us the central vision of Paul's completing ministry and of John's mending ministry. What is the vision? It is the all-inclusive, extensive, subjective Christ, who is the life-giving Spirit as the consummate expression of the Triune God now that He has accomplished all the processes. We must see Christ as such a One. We must live such a Christ. He must be our life,...our living,...our daily family life,...[and] our church life. (*The World Situation and God's Move*, pp. 79-80)

When the Lord's recovery came to this country, I had a strong burden as to what I should do....I had no liberty from Him to speak on

WEEK 1 — DAY 1

other subjects. From the beginning I have always been in the Lord's central lane, His focus for His economy. The Lord's recovery among us is absolutely different from any kind of reformation. We are not here for a recovery of any doctrine or any practice. Because of this, in the twenty years that I have been here with you all, I have given messages only on the central lane, on the focus.

Because of my observation, I have become really burdened for some of the churches. It seems some of you do not have the clear vision about this. You may be satisfied just to have a church raised up. There is a danger ahead. If the elders lack a clear vision as to what the Lord is doing—and this vision must be very strong—we are doing things in vain.

In the New Testament in the first four books there is the one Christ. Then out of this Christ the apostles are produced. Then these apostles are the ones who bring the churches into being. One Christ produces the apostles, and the many apostles produce the churches.

After the twelve apostles, more were added, especially Paul. Timothy and all the co-workers were also added. In 2 Corinthians 4:1 Paul says, "Having this ministry as we have been shown mercy, we do not lose heart." "We" refers to the apostles and their co-workers; they, plural, have received this ministry, singular.…The ministry of righteousness and the ministry of the Spirit is…one [2 Cor. 3:7-11].…[This ministry is unique] because God is unique. His plan is unique. His work is unique. His way to carry out His work is unique. And the very instrument used for His way is the ministry.…In the New Testament, there is the unique Christ, the unique way, and the unique focus to carry out the unique circumference, the church, by the unique ministry.…The Lord's recovery is… unique in everything. It has the unique God, the unique plan, the unique economy, the unique work, the unique way, [the unique word], the unique Lord, the unique focus, and the unique ministry. (*Practical Talks to the Elders*, pp. 7-8, 56-57, 59)

Further Reading: Practical Talks to the Elders, chs. 2, 4

Enlightenment and inspiration: _____

_____

_____

_____

Morning Nourishment

Eph. **That He would grant you, according to the riches**
3:16-17 **of His glory, to be strengthened with power through**
His Spirit into the inner man, that Christ may
make His home in your hearts through faith...
19 **...That you may be filled unto all the fullness of God.**

As symbolized by the golden lampstand, the church is the
embodiment of the Triune God to express Him. As members of
Christ, we are sons of God born of Him, having His life and possessing His nature. Now we are learning to live by this life and
nature that we may be filled and saturated with the processed
Triune God to become His corporate expression through the
sevenfold, intensified Spirit.

The lampstands in Revelation 1, among whom Christ as the
Son of Man is walking, are identical. In the positive sense as
the testimony of Jesus, the lampstands should not be different.
Jesus does not have different testimonies. He has only one testimony—the testimony of the Triune God. (*The Conclusion of
the New Testament*, pp. 2344-2345)

Today's Reading

To say that the church is the embodiment of the Triune God
is not to make the church a part of deity or an object of worship.
...The church is an entity born of God (John 1:12-13), possessing God's life (1 John 5:11-12) and enjoying God's nature (2 Pet.
1:4). The church has the divine substance, bears the likeness of
Christ, and expresses God....Now we may enjoy this life and
nature day by day and learn to live not by our natural life but
by the divine life and nature. As we live this way and are transformed, there will be the fullness, the expression, the form, the
appearance of Christ...and we shall shine by the sevenfold,
intensified Spirit. (*The Conclusion of the New Testament*, p. 2344)

In the New Testament the fullness is the expression
through the completeness of the riches. This is the reason
that...Paul speaks of the unsearchable riches of Christ and
...of the fullness of Christ [Eph. 3:8; 1:23; 4:13]. The riches of

Christ are the various aspects of what Christ is, and the fullness of Christ is the result, the issue, of our enjoyment of these riches. As we enjoy the riches of Christ, these riches are assimilated into our being metabolically. Then they constitute us into the fullness of Christ, into the Body of Christ, the church, as His expression.

We all need to see the vision of how the church is constituted....Every fiber of our being needs to be strengthened into our inner man...so that the indwelling Christ can spread Himself throughout our being and make His home in our inward parts. As Christ spreads within us, He saturates every area of our inner being metabolically with all that He is. Then we are rooted and grounded in love, we lay hold of the dimensions of Christ, and we know His love that surpasses knowledge. Then, ultimately, we are filled unto the fullness of God which is the church.

In the light of such a vision we see that it is utterly wrong to regard the church as a material building where "services" are held. It is also not adequate to view the church merely as the *ekklesia*, the gathering together of God's called-out people. Although many Christians today use the term "the Body of Christ," few have any clear realization of what this term signifies. The Body of Christ is the expression of Christ....[and] the fullness of Christ, which is the fullness of God. This fullness of God comes into existence in a practical way by our being strengthened into the inner man, by Christ making His home in our hearts, by our being rooted and grounded in love, by our grasping the dimensions of the immeasurable Christ, and by our knowing Him as the knowledge-surpassing love. When we have been filled with all the riches of Christ and metabolically saturated with all that Christ is, we become the fullness of God. (*Life-study of Ephesians,* pp. 294-295)

Further Reading: Life-study of Ephesians, msg. 34; *The Divine Economy,* ch. 14

Enlightenment and inspiration: _____

_____

_____

Morning Nourishment

Rev. Saying, What you see write in a scroll and send *it* to
1:11 the seven churches...

12 And I turned to see the voice that spoke with me;
and when I turned, I saw seven golden lampstands.

20 The mystery of the seven stars which you saw
upon My right hand and the seven golden lampstands: The seven stars are the messengers of the
seven churches, and the seven lampstands are
the seven churches.

Paul prayed that the Father would strengthen the believers
with power through the Spirit into the inner man so that Christ
the Son could make His home in the believers....so that they
might be filled unto all the fullness of the Triune God [Eph. 3:16-
19]. The Father strengthens through the Spirit so that the Son
could make home. This is the Triune God getting Himself fully
settled in your inner being to fill your mind and emotion and
will, and even to fill every corner of your conscience and heart
and spirit. He wants to fill you so that every part of your entire
being might be filled unto overflowing with the Triune God. This
is the reality of God's expression.

What [the Lord] wants to recover is that the Father would
strengthen us through the Spirit into our inner man, that the
Son, the all-inclusive One, might make His home and get Himself fully settled into our heart, into every part of our inner being,
so that our whole being will be filled unto the overflowing of the
Triune God to become an expression of God. (*Concerning the
Lord's Recovery,* p. 64)

Today's Reading

The Body of Christ, the church, is four-in-one: the Father, the
Son, the Spirit, and the Body. Ephesians 4:4-6 speaks of one
Body, one Spirit, one Lord, and one God the Father. In the Body
the Spirit is the essence. The essence needs the element, which
is the Lord Christ. The element must have an origin, a source,
which is the Father. The Father is the source, the origin. Out of

the Father there is the element, and within the element there is the essence. God is the origin, the Son is the element, the Spirit is the essence, and the Body is the very constitution. These are four-in-one. However, only the first three are worthy of our worship; the fourth, the Body, should not be deified as an object of worship.

The Spirit as the oneness of the Body of Christ is the essence of the Body to consummate the mingling of the Triune God with the Body of Christ through the divine dispensing. Today something is going on to mingle the Father as the origin, the Son as the element, and the Spirit as the essence with the Body. This mingling is continuing today and will be consummated. The Spirit is the essence of the Body to consummate this mingling. (*The Central Line of the Divine Revelation,* pp. 127-128)

The local churches, composed with the believers to be the Body of Christ, are the golden lampstands (Rev. 1:11-12). The lampstands are a testimony.

All the golden lampstands are identical in nature, in shape, and in function to be the one expression of Christ. If the seven lampstands were put before us, we would not be able to distinguish them, because they are identical. Without numbering them, no one could discern which lampstand is which. They all are identical in their golden nature, the divine nature, in their shape, the form of Christ, and in their function, the shining of the Spirit. The Father is the nature, the Son is the shape, the form, and the Spirit is the shining power. All the local churches should be identical in the same nature of God, form of Christ, and function of the Spirit.

The Body of Christ is the organism of the Triune God in His move. Life is a substance, the Triune God, and the organism is the visible expression of this substance. (*The Ten Great Critical "Ones" for the Building Up of the Body of Christ,* pp. 59-60)

Further Reading: Concerning the Lord's Recovery, ch. 5; *The Ten Great Critical "Ones" for the Building Up of the Body of Christ,* ch. 6*

Enlightenment and inspiration: ___4 in 1___

in the ⎰ Spirit - essence
Body ⎱ Son - element
　　　 Father - source, origin

Morning Nourishment

Rev. Who testified the word of God and the testimony of
1:2 Jesus Christ, *even* all that he saw.
9 I John, your brother and fellow partaker in the
tribulation and kingdom and endurance in Jesus,
was on the island called Patmos because of the
word of God and the testimony of Jesus.

As golden lampstands, the churches shine in the darkness. The word "lampstand" enables us to understand much about the church and its function....Without the lamp, the lampstand is vain and means nothing....Christ is the lamp (Rev. 21:23), and the church is the lampstand holding the lamp. God is in Christ, and Christ as the lamp is held by the stand to shine out God's glory. This is the testimony of the church. (*The Conclusion of the New Testament*, pp. 2341)

Today's Reading

The churches as golden lampstands bear the testimony of Jesus. "The testimony of Jesus" (Rev. 1:2, 9; 20:4) is an all-inclusive expression. The testimony of Jesus is the testimony of the Son coming with the Father by the Spirit to live on earth, to die on the cross to clear up the universe, to release the divine life, and to resurrect from the dead to become the life-giving Spirit, who then comes as the Son with the Father compounded with divinity, humanity, human living, crucifixion, and resurrection, including all the divine attributes and the human virtues....This testimony has a symbol—the golden lampstand. The golden lampstand is the testimony of Jesus.

The lampstands shine in the darkness. If there were no darkness, there would be no need for the shining of the light of the lamp....In order for the lamp to shine, it must have oil burning within it. If the oil burns within the lamp, the light will shine out through all the darkness. This is the function of the church....In the dark night of this age, the church must shine out the glory of God. (*The Conclusion of the New Testament*, pp. 2341-2342)

The church is not only universally one, but also expressed locally in many cities. In the whole universe there is only one Christ, one Spirit, and one church....[There are seven churches] because of the need for an expression. For existence, one is sufficient. But for expression, many are needed. If we would know the church, we must know its substance, existence, and expression. Substantially, the church, and even all the churches, are one. In expression, the many churches are the many lampstands....The church is the expression of the Triune God, and this expression is seen in many localities on earth....In Revelation 1 there are seven lampstands with forty-nine lamps shining in the universe.   49

The church is the expression of the Triune God substantially and expressively. Substantially, it is of one substance in the whole universe; expressively, it is many lampstands with the lamps shining in the darkness to express the Triune God. The Father as the substance is embodied in the Son, the Son as the embodiment is expressed through the Spirit, the Spirit is fully realized and reproduced as the churches, and the churches are the testimony of Jesus. If we see this vision, it will govern us, and we shall never be divisive.

The lampstand is the divine gold embodied into a substantial form to fulfill God's purpose in His move. The expression of the stand is in the shining of the light. As the expression shines, the shining fulfills God's eternal purpose. Thus, the lampstand signifies not only the Triune God, but also the move of the Triune God in His embodiment and expression....We should not be satisfied with saying that the local churches are the lampstands shining in the dark night. Although this is correct, it is rather shallow. We must see that the local churches are the reproduction of the embodiment and expression of the Triune God. (*The Genuine Ground of Oneness,* pp. 130-131)

Further Reading: The Genuine Ground of Oneness, ch. 10; *Lifestudy of Revelation,* msg. 8

Enlightenment and inspiration: The golden lampstard is the testimony of Jesus.

Morning Nourishment

2 Pet. **Through which He has granted to us precious and**
1:4 **exceedingly great promises that through these you**
might become partakers of the divine nature...
Col. **For in Him dwells all the fullness of the Godhead**
2:9 **bodily.**
Rev. **...*There were* seven lamps of fire burning before**
4:5 **the throne, which are the seven Spirits of God.**

Both in Exodus and Zechariah the lampstand is uniquely
one. But in Revelation, the book of consummation, there are
seven lampstands signifying seven local churches (Rev. 1:11-
12, 20b). This indicates that Christ as signified by the lampstand in Exodus and the Spirit of God as signified by the seven
lamps of the lampstand in Zechariah are for the reproduction
of the local churches. One lampstand is reproduced in the
seven lampstands....All the local churches as the many lampstands are the reproduction of Christ and the Spirit as the one
lampstand. This reproduction is actually a multiplication of
the wonderful expression of Christ as the life-giving Spirit in
a practical way.

In Exodus 25 the emphasis is on the stand—on Christ. In
Zechariah the emphasis is on the lamps—on the Spirit. Eventually, in Revelation both the stand and the lamps, that is,
both Christ and the Spirit, are reproduced as the local churches. The lampstands with their lamps in Revelation are the
reproduction of Christ and the Spirit. (*The Conclusion of the
New Testament*, pp. 2339-2340)

Today's Reading

In the golden lampstand there are three main factors: the
substance, the shape or form, and the expression. The substance, the material, of the lampstand is gold, which signifies
the Father's divine essence.

There was no dross in the lampstand, for it was made of pure
gold. In typology, dross signifies something other than God
brought in to cause a mixture....We should not bring anything

other than God into the church life. Even good things such as ethics, culture, education, and proper religion are dross, because they are not God Himself. Only God, the divine Being, is the gold which is the substance of the lampstand.

All the local churches are divine in nature; they are constituted of the divine essence....The local churches must be divine. Without divinity, there can be no church. Although the church is composed of humanity with divinity, humanity should not be the basic nature of the local churches...[but] divinity.

The golden lampstand is not a lump of gold but gold in a definite form and purposeful shape. The form, the shape, of the lampstand signifies the Son's human form. Christ, the Son, is the embodiment of the Godhead, the embodiment of the Father's nature (Col. 2:9). Therefore, the church should have not only the Father's divine essence but also the Son's human form.

The fact that the form of the lampstand signifies the Son as the embodiment of the Godhead indicates that the church should not be vague but should have a definite shape....The Lord Jesus, as the embodiment of the invisible God, was clearly standing as He spoke to the churches. All the churches should also stand, having the Son's shape.

Furthermore, the golden lampstands as the testimony of Jesus have the Spirit's expression. The seven lamps of the lampstand shine for God's expression. These seven lamps are the seven Spirits of God. Thus, with the lampstand are the Father's essence, the Son's human form, and the Spirit's expression. Since the golden lampstand has these three aspects, we can say that the golden lampstand signifies the embodiment of the Triune God, with the Father as the substance, the Son as the form, and the Spirit as the expression. (*The Conclusion of the New Testament,* pp. 2342-2344)

Further Reading: The Conclusion of the New Testament, msgs. 219-220

Enlightenment and inspiration: _____

_____

_____

_____

Morning Nourishment

1 Tim. Holding the mystery of the faith in a pure con-
3:9   science.
15 But if I delay, *I write* that you may know how one
ought to conduct himself in the house of God,
which is the church of the living God, the pillar
and base of the truth.

God's center in His economy has been revealed and written
in the Scriptures for close to two thousand years. Through all
these centuries quite a few books have been published to
unfold this mystery. Yet very few of even the lovers, the seek-
ers, of the Lord have really seen this and lived a life for this. It
is hard to find Christians who are really in this focus.

The churches in the United States have been in existence
for quite some time. Most were not raised up recently....As far
as the actual and practical church life is concerned, I am burdened that there is not much evidence that the churches are
such a testimony to God's economy. I do not mean that in
every meeting we talk only about the central lane, the focus,
God's economy. But I mean that we have a church life which is
a testimony to what Paul calls the mystery of the faith. (*Practical Talks to the Elders,* pp. 9-10)

Today's Reading

Have you really seen a vision of God's eternal purpose, a
vision of God's economy, of what God wants?

I have been fighting for Christ being the Spirit and for the
Triune God being not for doctrine but for experience....I do
not [speak of] this from habit. If I were only a Bible teacher, I
have sixty-six books from which to teach. But the Lord has
shown me that this would not be of His desire.

In Revelation...the lampstands represent the Triune God
with the Father as the nature, the Son as the embodiment,
and the Spirit as the expression. This is the church....And this
should be the very essence of the church's shining.

[The light and the testimony that the church shines forth]...

must be the Triune God. I do not say that in every meeting this is the subject. But whatever we fellowship about, whatever we minister, there must be such a testimony. In everything we do—gospel preaching, Bible teaching, visiting the saints, and even visiting new ones not yet saved—we must bear a clear, evident, strong testimony of a lampstand constituted of the Father's nature, the Son's embodiment, and the Spirit's expression....We must bear such a testimony in every aspect of the church life and of our daily life, including the family life.

To bear such a testimony is to hold the mystery of the faith. "Mystery" here does not denote a doctrine; even the word "faith" does not mean doctrine here....The faith is the reality of the content of the New Testament economy of God in which we believe. Our belief is not in doctrines but in such a reality. Of this faith, which is the content of God's New Testament economy, there is a mystery. In using this word mystery, Paul refers first to Christ as the mystery of God (Col. 2:2) and second to the church as the mystery of Christ (Eph. 3:4-6). According to the context of 1 Timothy 3:9, the mystery of the faith should also include the church life (cf. v. 16). Why? Because the church life is constituted of God in Christ and of Christ as the life-giving Spirit. This corresponds to the constitution of the lampstand. As the lampstand is constituted of the Father, the Son, and the Spirit, so the church also is constituted of the divine Trinity.

The church life is not something organized....It is a living organism constituted of the living God in His divine Trinity—the Father's nature, the Son's embodiment, and the Spirit's expression. This is not only the church; it is also the church life, the church's living. Thus it is a golden lampstand shining out the testimony of the Triune God. (*Practical Talks to the Elders,* pp. 10-11)

Further Reading: Practical Talks to the Elders, ch. 1; *Life-study of Exodus,* msg. 92

Enlightenment and inspiration: _____

_____

_____

_____

Hymns, #1220

1   Remove the veils, Lord, from my heart;
      True revelation grant to me;
      A vision clear, O Lord, impart
      Of Thy recovery.

2   By revelation I perceive
      The power that raised Christ from the dead;
      When I by faith this power receive,
      I to the church am led.

3   Thy mighty power has set me free
      From all the world's distracting things;
      An entrance to the local church
      This mighty power brings.

4   Once in the local church, I need
      To take Thee as my person, Lord;
      My outward man each day recede,
      My heart is for the Lord.

5   I take Thee as my person, Lord;
      I have been crucified with Thee.
      My inner man has been restored;
      I'm now indwelt by Thee.

6   When all Thy members self forsake,
      Thy glorious Body, Lord, is known;
      When of Thy Person we partake,
      The one new man is shown.

7   The church life is the one new man
      In every local church expressed;
      Thy Body is a corporate man,
      One Person manifest.

(Repeat the last two lines of each stanza)

Composition for prophecy with main point and sub-points: _____

_____
_____
_____
_____
_____
_____
_____
_____
_____
_____
_____
_____
_____
_____
_____
_____
_____
_____
_____
_____
_____
_____
_____
_____
_____
_____
_____
_____
_____
_____
_____
_____

The Focus of the Epistles—the Divine Trinity for the Divine Dispensing

Scripture Reading: Rom. 8:9, 11; 1 Cor. 12:4-6; 2 Cor. 13:14; Gal. 4:4-6; Eph. 2:18; 2 Thes. 2:13-14; Titus 3:4-6; 1 Pet. 1:2; Jude 20-21

Day 1

I. **The Divine Trinity is the focus of the Epistles (Rom. 8:9, 11; 1 Cor. 12:4-6; 2 Cor. 13:14; Gal. 4:4-6; Eph. 2:18; 2 Thes. 2:13-14; Titus 3:4-6; Jude 20-21):**

A. "The love of God has been poured out in our hearts through the Holy Spirit, who has been given to us. For while we were yet weak, in due time Christ died for the ungodly" (Rom. 5:5-6):

1. Christ the Son died for us, the Spirit has been given to us, and through this Spirit the love of God has been poured out in our hearts (vv. 5-6).

2. Now we enjoy the love of God through the Holy Spirit given to us on the foundation of the death of Christ for us, the ungodly.

B. "You are not in the flesh, but in the spirit, if indeed the Spirit of God dwells in you. Yet if anyone does not have the Spirit of Christ, he is not of Him" (8:9):

1. Here *the Spirit of God* and *the Spirit of Christ* are used interchangeably, indicating that the indwelling Spirit of life (v. 2) is the all-inclusive life-giving Spirit of the entire Triune God.

2. God, the Spirit, and Christ—the three of the Godhead—are all mentioned in this verse; however, there is only one in us, the triune Spirit of the Triune God (John 4:24; 2 Cor. 3:17; Rom. 8:11):

   a. *The Spirit of God* implies that the Spirit is of the One who was from eternity past, who created the universe and is the origin of all things.

   b. *The Spirit of Christ* implies that the Spirit is the embodiment and reality of Christ, the incarnated One, who accomplished everything necessary to fulfill God's plan (v. 3).

3. God the Father, Christ the Son, and God the Spirit are dwelling in us, making Their home in us; we have this wonderful triune Occupant inside of us (v. 11; cf. Eph. 3:16-17).

C. "If the Spirit of the One who raised Jesus from the dead dwells in you, He who raised Christ from the dead will also give life to your mortal bodies through His Spirit who indwells you" (Rom. 8:11):

1. In this verse we have the entire Triune God: "the One who raised Jesus from the dead," "Christ," and "His Spirit who indwells you."

2. In this verse we also have the process required for the divine dispensing, God's dispensing of Himself, into the believers:

   a. The process is implied in the words *Jesus* (emphasizing incarnation), *Christ* (emphasizing crucifixion and resurrection), and *raised* (emphasizing resurrection).

   b. The divine dispensing is shown by the words *give life to your mortal bodies*.

D. "That I might be a minister of Christ Jesus to the Gentiles, a laboring priest of the gospel of God, in order that the offering of the Gentiles might be acceptable, having been sanctified in the Holy Spirit" (15:16):

1. Paul said that he was a minister of Christ Jesus, the Son, to the Gentiles, ministering as a priest the gospel of the Triune God so that the offering of the Gentiles might be acceptable, having been sanctified in the Holy Spirit.

2. Paul was a laboring priest of the gospel of the Triune God, ministering Christ Jesus, the Son, to the Gentiles; eventually, the result of his work was to offer the Gentiles to God as a sanctified entity through the Holy Spirit.

II. **Everything that is mentioned concerning the Divine Trinity in the New Testament is related to the divine dispensing (1 Pet. 1:2; 2 Thes. 2:13-14):**

Day 4

A. The revelation of the Divine Trinity in the holy Word is not for mere doctrinal understanding but for the dispensing of the Triune God in His Divine Trinity into His chosen and redeemed people for their experience, enjoyment, and growth in life (2 Cor. 13:14).

Day 5

B. The crucial focus of Ephesians is the divine dispensing of the Divine Trinity into the believers:

   1. Chapter 1 unveils how God the Father chose and predestinated the members in eternity, God the Son redeemed them, and God the Spirit sealed them as a pledge, thus imparting Himself into His believers for the formation of the church, which is the Body of Christ, the fullness of the One who fills all in all (vv. 3-14, 17-23).

   2. Chapter 2 shows us that in the Divine Trinity all the believers, both Jewish and Gentile, have access unto God the Father, through God the Son, in God the Spirit (v. 18).

   3. In chapter 3 the apostle prays that God the Father would grant the believers to be strengthened through God the Spirit into their inner man so that Christ, God the Son, may make His home in their hearts, that they may be filled unto all the fullness of God (vv. 16-19).

   4. Chapter 4 portrays how the processed God as the Spirit, the Lord, and the Father is mingled with the Body of Christ so that all the members of the Body may experience the Divine Trinity (vv. 4-6).

   5. Chapter 5 exhorts the believers to praise the Lord, God the Son, with the songs of God the Spirit, and give thanks in the name of our

Lord Jesus Christ, God the Son, to God the Father (vv. 19-20).

6. Chapter 6 instructs us to fight the spiritual warfare by being empowered in the Lord, God the Son, putting on the whole armor of God the Father, and wielding the sword of the Spirit (vv. 10-11, 17).

Day 6

C. In our daily living we need to receive, experience, and enjoy the divine dispensing in a normal, gradual, and steady way (Rom. 8:11; 2 Cor. 13:14):

1. The more we experience the divine dispensing, the more we grow in life for the building up of the Body of Christ (Eph. 3:16-19; 4:15-16).

2. The processed and consummated Triune God is within us not in a spectacular way but in an ordinary way (Rom. 8:9, 11):

   a. We need to live a life in the divine dispensing in a normal way and learn to be satisfied with ordinary days in the divine dispensing.

   b. Our destiny is to live a normal life in the divine dispensing; it is a blessing to be satisfied with ordinary days in the divine dispensing.

Morning Nourishment

Rom. ...The love of God has been poured out in our hearts
5:5-6 through the Holy Spirit, who has been given to us.
For while we were yet weak, in due time Christ died
for the ungodly.
8:9 But you are not in the flesh, but in the spirit, if
indeed the Spirit of God dwells in you. Yet if anyone
does not have the Spirit of Christ, he is not of Him.

The entire book of Ephesians is composed with the Trinity
as its basic structure; every chapter, from one through six, is
constructed in this way....Second Corinthians 13:14 also indicates the Trinity when it says, "The grace of the Lord Jesus
Christ and the love of God and the fellowship of the Holy
Spirit be with you all." Consider also the Trinity unveiled in
the first few verses of Revelation. The entire Bible gives us a
complete revelation of the Divine Trinity. This revelation is
the focus of the Epistles. Even Revelation is an epistle, written to the seven churches. The Divine Trinity, then, is the
focus of the Epistles. (*Practical Talks to the Elders,* p. 56)

Today's Reading

The Epistles show us the unique focus of God's economy
What is this unique focus?....You may say that Christ is the
unique focus of God's economy,...[but it] is not merely Christ.
Of course, it depends on how you define the term Christ.

Colossians 2:9 says, "In Him dwells all the fullness of the
Godhead bodily."...[This verse] says "the fullness of the Godhead," not the fullness of God. Godhead means God Himself.
The Godhead is triune. That the fullness of the Godhead
dwells in Christ really denotes that the Divine Trinity is
dwelling in Christ in full. The fullness of the Trinity dwells in
Him bodily....The expression...,the fullness of the Godhead, is
a strong one, telling us that the fullness of the Trinity dwells
in this One bodily. If we say that Christ is the focus of the New
Testament, then, our understanding of Christ must include
the realization that in this One is the fullness of the Trinity.

It is such a Christ that is the focus of the New Testament. (*Practical Talks to the Elders,* pp. 54-55)

Romans 5:5 and 6 show the love of God [God the Father] having been poured out in our hearts through the Holy Spirit given to us and Christ [the Son] having died for the ungodly. The pouring out of God's love was carried out through the Holy Spirit whom God has given to us....First, the Son died for us, the ungodly. Based upon this the Spirit was given to us, and through this Spirit given to us, the love of God has been poured out in our hearts. Now we enjoy the love of God through the Holy Spirit given to us on the foundation of the death of Christ for us, the ungodly. (*Living in and with the Divine Trinity,* pp. 70-71)

The Spirit of God and the Spirit of Christ are not two Spirits but one. Paul used these titles interchangeably, indicating that the indwelling Spirit of life in [Romans] 8:2 is the all-inclusive, life-giving Spirit of the entire Triune God. God, the Spirit, and Christ—the three of the Godhead—are all mentioned in verse 9. However, there are not three in us; there is only one, the triune Spirit of the Triune God (John 4:24; 2 Cor. 3:17; Rom. 8:11). *The Spirit of God* implies that this Spirit is of the One who was from eternity past, who created the universe and is the origin of all things. *The Spirit of Christ* implies that this Spirit is the embodiment and reality of Christ, the incarnated One. This is the Spirit of Christ in resurrection, that is, Christ Himself dwelling in our spirit (v. 10) to impart Himself, the embodiment of the processed Triune God, into us as resurrection life and power to deal with the death that is in our nature (v. 2). Thus, we may live today in Christ's resurrection, in Christ Himself, by living in the mingled spirit. (*Crystallization-study of the Complete Salvation of God in Romans,* pp. 22-23)

Further Reading: Living in and with the Divine Trinity, chs. 6-9; *Practical Talks to the Elders,* ch. 4

Enlightenment and inspiration: _____

_____
_____
_____

Morning Nourishment

Eph. That He would grant you, according to the riches of
3:16-17 His glory, to be strengthened with power through
His Spirit into the inner man, that Christ may make
His home in your hearts through faith...

Rom ...If the Spirit of the One who raised Jesus from
8:11 the dead dwells in you, He who raised Christ
from the dead will also give life to your mortal
bodies through His Spirit who indwells you.

Romans 8:9 speaks of the Spirit of God [the Father] dwelling in us and also speaks of the Spirit of Christ [the Son]. The Spirit of God and the Spirit of Christ are not two Spirits. They are one Spirit in two aspects. The Spirit of God is the Spirit of Christ....God and Christ being one is shown by the fact that the Spirit is the Spirit of both God and Christ. God the Father, Christ the Son, and God the Spirit are in us. They are indwelling us, making Their home in us. We have a wonderful Occupant inside of us, a triune Occupant. Romans 8:9 shows us the beauty of the Three of the Divine Trinity working together for our benefit. (*Living in and with the Divine Trinity*, p. 55)

Today's Reading

Paul prayed that God would give us a spirit of wisdom and revelation that we might know Him and His economy (Eph. 1:17). He prayed that we would have the ability, the power, to see the spiritual revelation. In chapter 1 his prayer is for our seeing the vision, but in chapter 3 his prayer is for our experience of the depths of Christ.

First, Paul prayed to the Father as the source. Then the Father strengthens the believers through the Spirit as the means, the channel. Then Christ moves and works to make His home in the believers' hearts. Eventually, the issue of the moving of the Father and the Spirit, and of the Son making His home in our hearts is the fullness of the Triune God. The Father is the source, the Spirit is the means, the Son is the object, and the fullness of the Triune God is the issue.

The source is the Father, the means is the Spirit, and the aim, the goal, is the Son because the Son is the center. Whatever the Triune God does is for the Son as the center, out of the Father as the source, and through the Spirit as the means. Paul prayed to the Father as the source, asking the Father to strengthen the believers through the channel of the Spirit that a goal might be reached. The goal was that Christ would make His home in the hearts of the believers.

This is a beautiful picture of the Divine Trinity in His deeper work within us...to make His home in our hearts. Our hearts are composed of the mind, the emotion, and the will, plus the conscience of our spirit. Christ is making His home in these four parts by the preparation made through the channel, the Spirit, as an answer to the apostle's prayer made to the source, the Father. Eventually, the Son becomes settled in each part of our heart. (*Living in and with the Divine Trinity,* pp. 57-60)

[In Romans 8:11] the Spirit of Christ is also the Spirit of the One who raised Jesus from among the dead, dwelling in us to give life to our mortal body....In this verse we have three matters. First, we have the entire Triune God—the One who raised Jesus from the dead, Christ Jesus, and His Spirit who indwells you. Second, we have the process required for His dispensing, as implied in the words *Jesus* (emphasizing incarnation), *Christ* (emphasizing crucifixion and resurrection), and *raised* (emphasizing resurrection). Third, we have His dispensing of Himself into the believers, as shown by the phrase *give life to your mortal bodies,* which indicates that the dispensing not only occurs at the center of our being but also reaches to the circumference, to our whole being. The phrase *give life to your mortal bodies* does not refer to divine healing but to the result of our allowing the Spirit of God to make His home in us and saturate our entire being with the divine life (Eph. 3:16-19). (*The Conclusion of the New Testament,* p. 3078)

Further Reading: Living in and with the Divine Trinity, chs. 3-5, 10-13

Enlightenment and inspiration: _____

_____

_____

_____

Morning Nourishment

Rom. That I might be a minister of Christ Jesus to the Gen-
15:16 tiles, a laboring priest of the gospel of God, in order
that the offering of the Gentiles might be acceptable,
having been sanctified in the Holy Spirit.

1 Pet. Chosen according to the foreknowledge of God the
1:2 Father in the sanctification of the Spirit unto the
obedience and sprinkling of the blood of Jesus
Christ: Grace to you and peace be multiplied.

In Romans 15:16 Paul said that he was a minister of Christ Jesus
[the Son] to the nations, ministering as a priest the gospel of [the Tri-
une] God, that the offering of the nations [the Gentiles] might be
acceptable, having been sanctified in the Holy Spirit. Paul was a
priest of the gospel of the Triune God, ministering Christ Jesus, the
Son, to the nations. Eventually, the result of his work was to offer the
nations to God as a sanctified entity through the Holy Spirit. (*Living
in and with the Divine Trinity,* p. 75)

Today's Reading

The words *economy* and *dispensing* are somewhat unfamiliar
and even peculiar terms to some of us. According to the New Testament revelation, *economy* is a particular term used by God to
unveil His eternal plan. In Greek this word is *oikonomia,* composed of two words, *oikos* and *nomos.* The word *oikos* means
house, family, or household, and the word *nomos* means law.
When we put the two words together, the result, *oikonomia,*
means a household regulation, household government, or household administration. Within a household administration there
are some plans and arrangements, and there is the exercise of
some kind of skill for the dispensing of the riches of the household
to the family members.

The word *dispensing* carries the denotation of distributing. In
a love feast we may have an abundance of food, but there is the
need for some "dispensers" to distribute the food to everyone. This
distributing of food is the dispensing of food. Furthermore, when
the food gets into us, it begins to dispense itself within us. Our

digestion of the food is our cooperation with the dispensing of the food. After digestion, there is also the process of assimilation, through which we assimilate what has been received through digestion. This is a further cooperation with the dispensing of the food. In this way, the food will be in us, and everything we have eaten will become part of us. This is the denotation and the connotation of the word *dispensing*.

The entire economy of God, and especially that in the New Testament age, is a matter of dispensing. I do not say that it is a matter of *dispensation*. The word *dispensation* conveys a different notion. I like to use the word *dispensing* as a noun in expressions such as *God's dispensing* or *the divine dispensing*. In the New Testament, God is carrying out His economy, His household administration, which He made in eternity past, before the foundation of the world. God's intention in His economy, His household government, is just to dispense Himself in His Divine Trinity—the Father, the Son, and the Spirit—into His chosen people....If we dive into the depth of the New Testament as the divine revelation, we will see that God surely has an economy, a household administration, to carry out His eternal purpose. This economy is just God's universal operation.

John 3:16...says, "For God so loved the world that He gave His only begotten Son, that everyone who believes into Him would not perish, but would have eternal life." In this verse three things are taking place: first, God gave, and is still giving; second, we believe; and third, we shall have eternal life. In these three points we can see God's dispensing. God's giving is a kind of dispensing. Suppose I have a lot of money, and I give each of you some of this money. My giving is my dispensing. I unload my money to you by the way of dispensing. God so loved the world that He *gave* His only begotten Son. This means that God is dispensing His Son to us. What God dispenses is not money, but His only begotten Son. (*The Economy and Dispensing of God*, pp. 69-71)

Further Reading: The Economy and Dispensing of God, chs. 7-10

Enlightenment and inspiration: _____

_____

_____

_____

Morning Nourishment

Matt. Go therefore and disciple all the nations, baptizing
28:19 them into the name of the Father and of the Son and
of the Holy Spirit.
2 Cor. The grace of the Lord Jesus Christ and the love of God
13:14 and the fellowship of the Holy Spirit be with you all.

The grace of the Lord is the Lord Himself as life to us for our enjoyment (John 1:17 and note1;1 Cor. 15:10 and note 1), the love of God is God Himself (1 John 4:8, 16) as the source of the grace of the Lord, and the fellowship of the Spirit is the Spirit Himself as the transmission of the grace of the Lord with the love of God for our participation. These are not three separate matters but three aspects of one thing, just as the Lord, God, and the Holy Spirit are not three separate Gods but three "hypostases...of the one same undivided and indivisible" God (Philip Schaff). The Greek word for *hypostasis* (used in Heb. 11:1—see note 2 there), the singular form of *hypostases*, refers to a support under, a support beneath, that is, something underneath that supports, a supporting substance. The Father, the Son, and the Spirit are the hypostases, the supporting substances, that compose the one Godhead. (Footnote 1 on 2 Corinthians 13:14)

Today's Reading

The love of God is the source, since God is the origin; the grace of the Lord is the course of the love of God, since the Lord is the expression of God; and the fellowship of the Spirit is the impartation of the grace of the Lord with the love of God, since the Spirit is the transmission of the Lord with God, for our experience and enjoyment of the Triune God— the Father, the Son, and the Holy Spirit, with Their divine virtues....Such a divine attribute of three virtues—love, grace, and fellowship— and such a Triune God of the three divine hypostases—the Father, the Son, and the Spirit—were needed by the distracted and confused yet comforted and restored Corinthian believers. Hence, the apostle used all these divine and precious things in one sentence to conclude his lovely and dear Epistle.

This verse is strong proof that the trinity of the Godhead is not for the doctrinal understanding of systematic theology but for the dispensing of God Himself in His trinity into His chosen and redeemed people. In the Bible the Trinity is never revealed merely as a doctrine. It is always revealed or mentioned in regard to the relationship of God with His creatures, especially with man, who was created by Him, and more particularly with His chosen and redeemed people. The first divine title used in the divine revelation, *Elohim* in Hebrew, a title used in relation to God's creation, is plural in number (Gen. 1:1), implying that God, as the Creator of the heavens and the earth for man, is triune. Concerning His creation of man in His own image, after His own likeness, He used the plural pronouns *Us* and *Our,* referring to His trinity (Gen. 1:26) and implying that He would be one with man and express Himself through man in His trinity. Later, in Genesis 3:22 and 11:7 and Isaiah 6:8, He referred to Himself again and again as *Us* in regard to His relationship with man and with His chosen people.

After His resurrection He charged His disciples to disciple the nations, baptizing them into the name of the Father and of the Son and of the Holy Spirit (Matt. 28:19); that is, He charged the disciples to bring the believing ones into the Triune God, into an organic union with the processed God, who had passed through incarnation, human living, and crucifixion and had entered into resurrection. Based on such an organic union, the apostle, at the conclusion of this divine Epistle to the Corinthians, blessed them with the blessed Divine Trinity in the participation in the Son's grace with the Father's love through the Spirit's fellowship. In this Divine Trinity, God the Father operates all things in all the members in the church, which is the Body of Christ, through the ministries of the Lord, God the Son, by the gifts of God the Spirit (1 Cor. 12:4-6). (Footnote 1 on 2 Corinthians 13:14)

Further Reading: The Economy and Dispensing of God, chs. 2-6

Enlightenment and inspiration: _____

_____

_____

Morning Nourishment

Eph. **And do not be drunk with wine, in which is disso-**
5:18-20 **luteness, but be filled in spirit, speaking to one**
another in psalms and hymns and spiritual songs,
...giving thanks at all times for all things in the name
of our Lord Jesus Christ to *our* God and Father.

The entire divine revelation in the book of Ephesians concerning the producing, existing, growing, building up, and fighting of
the church as the Body of Christ is composed of the divine economy,
the dispensing of the Triune God into the members of the Body of
Christ. Chapter 1 of Ephesians unveils that God the Father chose
and predestinated these members in eternity (1:4-5), that God the
Son redeemed them (1:6-12), and that God the Spirit, as a pledge,
sealed them (1:13-14), thus imparting Himself into His believers
for the formation of the church, which is the Body of Christ, the fullness of the One who fills all in all (1:18-23). (Footnote 1 on 2 Corinthians 13:14)

Today's Reading

Ephesians 2 shows us that in the Divine Trinity all the believers, both Jewish and Gentile, have access unto God the Father,
through God the Son, in God the Spirit (2:18). This indicates that
the three coexist and coinhere simultaneously, even after all the
processes of incarnation, human living, crucifixion, and resurrection. In chapter 3 the apostle prayed that God the Father would
grant the believers to be strengthened through God the Spirit into
their inner man, that Christ, God the Son, may make His home in
their hearts, that is, occupy their entire being, that they may be
filled unto all the fullness of God (3:14-19). This is the climax of the
believers' experience of and participation in God in His trinity.
Chapter 4 portrays how the processed God as the Spirit, the Lord,
and the Father is mingled with the Body of Christ (4:4-6) so that all
the members of the Body may experience the Divine Trinity. Chapter 5 exhorts the believers to praise the Lord, God the Son, with the
songs of God the Spirit, and give thanks in the name of our Lord
Jesus Christ, God the Son, to God the Father (5:19-20). This is to

praise and thank the processed God in His divine trinity for our enjoyment of Him as the Triune God. Chapter 6 instructs us to fight the spiritual warfare by being empowered in the Lord, God the Son, putting on the whole armor of God the Father, and wielding the sword of God the Spirit (6:10, 11, 17). This is the believers' experience and enjoyment of the Triune God even in the spiritual warfare.

The apostle Peter, in his writing, confirmed that God is triune for the believers' enjoyment, referring the believers to the election of God the Father, the sanctification of God the Spirit, and the redemption of Jesus Christ, God the Son, accomplished by His blood (1 Pet. 1:2). And John the apostle strengthened the revelation that the Divine Trinity is for the believers' participation in the processed Triune God. In the book of Revelation he blessed the churches in different localities with grace and peace from God the Father, Him who is and who was and who is coming, and from God the Spirit, the seven Spirits who are before His throne, and from God the Son, Jesus Christ, the faithful Witness, the Firstborn of the dead, and the Ruler of the kings of the earth (Rev. 1:4-5). John's blessing given to the churches indicated also that the processed Triune God, in all He is as the eternal Father, in all He is able to do as the sevenfold intensified Spirit, and in all He has attained and obtained as the anointed Son, is for the believers' enjoyment, that they may be His corporate testimony as the golden lampstands (1:9, 11, 20).

Thus, it is evident that the divine revelation of the trinity of the Godhead in the holy Word, from Genesis through Revelation, is not for theological study but for the apprehending of how God in His mysterious and marvelous trinity dispenses Himself into His chosen people, that we as His chosen and redeemed people may, as indicated in the apostle's blessing to the Corinthian believers, participate in, experience, enjoy, and possess the processed Triune God now and for eternity. Amen. (Footnote 1 on 2 Corinthians 13:14)

Further Reading: The Divine Dispensing of the Divine Trinity, chs. 15-20

__Enlightenment and inspiration:__ _____

_____

_____

_____

Morning Nourishment

Eph. But holding to truth in love, we may grow up into
4:15-16 Him in all things, who is the Head, Christ, out from
whom all the Body, being joined together and
being knit together through every joint of the rich
supply and *through* the operation in the measure
of each one part, causes the growth of the Body
unto the building up of itself in love.

The divine dispensing comes out of the Three of the Divine
Trinity—the Father, the Son, and the Spirit. The divine dispensing taking place within us is the operating of the all-
inclusive, life-giving Spirit, the pneumatic Christ, as the
aggregate, totality, and consummation of the Triune God.
This Spirit is moving in us, anointing us, watering us, feeding
us, satisfying us, strengthening us, comforting us, saturating
us, and permeating us. There are so many words to describe
His dispensing within us. All of the foregoing items, such as
watering, feeding, strengthening, permeating, saturating, and
anointing, are matters of dispensing. Every day we should be
built up by receiving the divine dispensing within us. (*The
Divine Dispensing for the Divine Economy*, p. 37)

Today's Reading

We should not expect to have a spectacular time each day
in receiving the divine dispensing....[We should not] expect to
have a spectacular result in [our] Christian life....We must
learn to be satisfied with ordinary days which are filled with
regular and normal practices in the divine dispensing. In the
morning we should have some time with the Lord to touch
Him and be revived by Him. Then we need to pass through a
daily routine to get ready for work. To live a life in the divine
dispensing in a normal way will make us healthy both physically and spiritually. Whether or not we have good or bad days
is not up to us; it is up to His sovereignty. He has already
chosen us, and it is too late to turn back. We are blessed
because the processed and consummated Triune God is

within us. He is in us, not in a spectacular way but in a very ordinary way.

We should be blessed to be satisfied with ordinary days in the divine dispensing. The Triune God is certainly in us, but His being in us is not spectacular. Every day He is within us dispensing and positively strengthening and encouraging us. In the last three years, I have experienced many troubles, yet nothing has disturbed me. I have published more messages, I have visited more places, and I have held more conferences. However, this is not because I have had spectacular days. I have just lived an ordinary life of receiving His dispensing. The Epistles reveal that the work of Christ within us is a fine work of dispensing....Our destiny is to live an ordinary life in the divine dispensing. Our Father God has destined that we live in an ordinary way under His continual dispensing.

Because all the riches of the Head have been dispensed into us, we grow with these riches in all things into the Head [Eph. 4:15]. Then out from the Head all the Body, joined closely together through every joint of the rich supply and knit together (interwoven) through the operation of each part in its measure, causes the growth of the Body, through the dispensing of the riches of the processed Triune God, unto the organic building up of the Body itself in love (v. 16).

It is by this thorough step-by-step dispensing that the Body grows and builds itself up. This is the dispensing of the consummated Triune God, the pneumatic Christ as the life-giving Spirit. He is anointing, moving, feeding, nourishing, strengthening, comforting, encouraging, and working within us. Every day we have to come back to the Spirit and remain in Him all the time. We must be one with the moving One within us. Then we will experience His fine work of divine dispensing. (*The Divine Dispensing for the Divine Economy*, pp. 37-40)

Further Reading: A Deeper Study of the Divine Dispensing, chs. 1-2, 7, 11-12

Enlightenment and inspiration: _____

_____

_____

_____

Hymns, #1321

1 The grace which God bestows on us
Is just His Son in full;
The rich enjoyment of this Christ
Is plenteous, bountiful.
'Tis far too great to comprehend,
Too wondrous to contain:
How we, once children of despair,
God's masterpiece became.

2 The whole creation now beneath
The weight of bondage sore,
In seeing God's sons manifest
Is freed forevermore.
Th' eternal purpose of our God
Will be full manifest;
The hope of glory now concealed
Is then to all expressed.

3 The briars will be myrtle trees,
The thorn will be no more,
And peace will reign where war did rage,
The curse will then be o'er.
'Tis then the trees shall clap their hands,
And all the hills shall sing;
This glorious freedom shall God's sons
Thus manifested bring.

4 God's deepest work of grace goes on
Each day, though hidden, small,
Until that day, when manifest,
It is revealed to all.
By then God's wrought His finished work:
Himself dispensed to us;
And all creation 'round admires
His product, glorious.

5 The angels that before our God
In brightest splendor stand,
Will join the universal praise
To Him for all He's planned.
And of the devil, of his end...?
We'll praise the Lord for how
Just distant smoke is all that's left
Of all that troubles now.

6   So shall we not delight to give
     Ourselves in every way,
     And let the Lord dispense Himself
     Into us more each day;
     The grace that we receive each day,
     Though hidden oft, and small,
     Is God Himself wrought into us,
     That day to shine o'er all.

Composition for prophecy with main point and sub-points: _____

_____

_____

_____

_____

_____

_____

_____

_____

_____

_____

_____

_____

_____

_____

_____

_____

_____

_____

_____

_____

_____

_____

_____

_____

_____

Romans 8—the Focus of the Entire Bible and the Center of the Universe

Scripture Reading: Rom. 8:2, 10, 4-6, 11, 13-15, 28-29

Day 1

I. Romans 8 reveals that the processed Triune God as the law of the Spirit of life gives the divine life to the believers for their living (vv. 2, 10, 6, 11, 28-29):

A. God's desire and goal are that we live by the divine life and minister life to others for the building up of the church; this life is in Christ Jesus, and it is the life of the law of the Spirit of life; the all-inclusive indwelling Spirit is constantly transmitting this life into each one of us to build up the church, edify the saints, and minister the riches of Christ to everyone who contacts us (v. 2; 2 Cor. 3:6; 1 John 5:16).

B. We need to see the way to live as a man by the law of the Spirit of life; we must be controlled and directed by the law of the Spirit of life to experience a genuine and normal Christian life (Rom. 8:2):

Day 2

1. We need to walk according to the spirit (v. 4):
   a. If we insist on anything for our own sake, interest, or profit, even if the thing itself is not sinful or immoral, we are walking according to the flesh.
   b. According to the Bible, there is no third choice or neutral ground; everything is either according to the flesh or the spirit (vv. 4, 6, 9; John 3:6; Gal. 5:17; 6:8; 1 Pet. 3:18).
   c. When we deduct the flesh, what remains is the spirit; since we know what the flesh is, we can walk according to the spirit simply by not walking according to the flesh.

2. We need to be according to the spirit (Rom. 8:5):
   a. A living according to the spirit and not according to the flesh is the realization of an inward law—the law of the Spirit of life (v. 2).

b. Being according to the flesh is like remaining on the ground according to the law of gravity, which may be likened to the law of sin and of death.

c. Being according to the spirit is like being on an airplane according to the law of aerodynamics, which may be likened to the law of the Spirit of life.

d. The law of the Spirit of life in our mingled spirit has the power to overcome the law of sin and of death in our flesh.

e. If we choose to be according to the spirit, the law of the Spirit of life will spontaneously free us from the law of sin and of death; the law of the Spirit of life does not need our help, but it needs our consent (cf. v. 6).

f. In every place and at every time, we need to build up a spiritual habit of exercising our spirit to "switch on" the law of the Spirit of life (1 Tim. 4:7).

g. The law of the Spirit of life, the Spirit of God, the Spirit of Christ, and the resurrecting Spirit have been installed into every believer; in order to receive His life supply, we need only to exercise our spirit by calling on the Lord and worshipping, thanking, praising, and exalting Him (Isa. 12:2-6).

Day 3

3. We need to mind the things of the Spirit (Rom. 8:5):

a. To mind the things of the Spirit is to set our mind on the things of the Spirit, that is, to always have our mind occupied with the things of the Spirit, which are the things concerning Christ.

b. The things of the Spirit of God are the deep things of God; to realize and participate in Christ as the deep things of God requires us to love Him (1 Cor. 2:9-11, 14).

    c. We need to exercise to build up a habit of continually having our mind occupied with the things of the Spirit, the things concerning Christ.

    d. In Song of Songs the seeker was sick with love for the Lord (2:5; 5:8); within her mind there was nothing but the Lord; we need to have such a mind.

    e. The secret of spiritual warfare is to not allow our mind to be vacant; the two spirits, the divine Spirit with our human spirit, connect all the things concerning Christ to our mind; as long as our mind is connected to the things concerning Christ by the two spirits, we are victorious (Rom. 8:6, 16).

    f. The expression *the mind set on the spirit* in Romans 8:6 is literally "the mind of the spirit"; the mind of Christ, the mind of the spirit, is a mind that is filled, occupied, and saturated with Christ (Phil. 2:5; 1 Cor. 2:16).

4. We need to put to death the practices of our body (Rom. 8:13, 5):

    a. The practices of the body are our old habits; these practices include not only sinful things but also everything practiced by our body apart from the Spirit.

    b. We need to coordinate with the indwelling Spirit to take the initiative to put to death the practices of our body; then the Spirit will come in to apply the effectiveness of Christ's death to these practices, thus killing them.

5. We need to be led by the Spirit of God (v. 14):

    a. We do not need to seek after the Spirit's leading, since it is already present within us, dwelling in our regenerated spirit; if we live under this leading, we will walk

and behave in a way that proves that we
are God's sons.

b. The leading here is not merely an action of
the Spirit; it is the Triune God Himself becoming the leading in our spirit; if we would
care for Him as a person who indwells us, we
will spontaneously be led by Him.

6. We need to cry, "Abba, Father!" (v. 15):

a. *Abba* is an Aramaic word, and *Father* is
the translation of the Greek word *Pater;*
the combining of the Aramaic title with the
Greek title expresses a stronger affection
in crying to the Father.

b. Such an affectionate cry implies an intimate relationship in life between a genuine son and a begetting father (v. 16).

Day 4 **II. Romans 8 may be considered the focus of the
entire Bible and the center of the universe;
thus, if we are experiencing Romans 8, we are
in the center of the universe:**

A. In eternity past God purposed to enter into His
redeemed people so that He could be their life and
so that they could be His corporate expression;
this is the focus of God's economy (Eph. 1:3-5).

B. Man is the center of God's creation, because God's
intention is to be expressed through man; man
can become God's expression only by God entering into man to be man's life and content and to
make man one with Him so that man may live by
Him and even live Him out; in this way God is
expressed from within man.

C. Zechariah 12:1 says, "Thus declares Jehovah, who
stretches forth the heavens and lays the founda-
tions of the earth and forms the spirit of man
within him":

1. The spirit of man is ranked with the heavens
and the earth because our spirit is the loca-
tion where God desires to dwell (Eph. 2:22;
cf. 2 Tim. 4:22).

   2. The heavens are for the earth, the earth is for man, and man was created by God with a spirit so that he may contact God, receive God, worship God, live God, fulfill God's purpose for God, and be one with God.

Day 5   D. The central focus in the universe is that the processed Triune God has come into us and now dwells in us; this is the greatest miracle; nothing else in the universe could be more important than this (Isa. 66:1-2; John 14:23; 15:4).

   E. We should all be full of joy since the Triune God is indwelling us and is one with us; He is our life and our person, and He is making us His home (Eph. 3:14-17). *inner man*

   F. The indwelling Spirit in Romans 8 is the Triune God:
   1. In the expression *the Spirit of God,* the Spirit and God are in apposition, indicating that the Spirit and God are one (Rom. 8:9).
   2. Similarly, *the Spirit of Christ, the Spirit of the One who raised Jesus from the dead,* and *the Spirit of life* in Romans 8 indicate that the Spirit is Christ, the resurrecting One, and life; therefore, since the Spirit indwells us, all three of the Triune God are in us as life (vv. 9, 11, 2).
   3. The Spirit in Romans 8 is the all-inclusive Spirit as the ultimate consummation and application of the Triune God; the Spirit is the reaching, the application, of the Triune God to us.
   4. The Triune God as the all-inclusive Spirit is within us for us to experience and enjoy by taking Him as our life and our person; we are the container of the Triune God (2 Cor. 4:7).

Day 6   G. When Christ enters into us, our spirit is regenerated, making our spirit life (Rom. 8:10); when we love the Lord and set our mind on the things concerning Him, our mind is life (v. 6); furthermore, if the Spirit of the resurrecting One indwells us, He will give life to our body (v. 11):

1. According to God's economy and eternal purpose, what God wants to do in His salvation is to work Himself into us, His redeemed people, as our life; God's desire to work Himself into us as our life is the focus of the Bible.
2. The life that is given to our spirit, mind, and body is the indwelling Spirit as the ultimate consummation and application of the Triune God.
3. If we are weak, lacking life, it is because we are short of spiritual breath; to breathe spiritually is to call on the name of the Lord (Lam. 3:55-56; *Hymns,* #73, stanza 2).
4. As we continually breathe in the Spirit as life and allow Him to spread into all our being, more and more of Christ is added into us; this is to possess, experience, and enjoy the subjective God within our being.
5. When God is thus added into our being, we will receive the life element that causes us to grow for the building up of the Body of Christ (Col. 2:19).
6. While we are growing with this life element, the law of the Spirit of life works in us automatically to shape us, to conform us, into the image of Christ; the Body of Christ, the fullness of Christ, the new man, and the mutual habitation of God and man issue from our experience of this life (Rom. 8:29).
7. Ultimately, this life will prepare the bride of Christ, which will cause the Lord to come back and usher us into the next age; for this reason, the crucial focus of the Bible and the universe is in Romans 8.

Morning Nourishment

Rom. For the law of the Spirit of life has freed me in Christ
8:2 Jesus from the law of sin and of death.
10-11 But if Christ is in you, though the body is dead because
of sin, the spirit is life because of righteousness. And if
the Spirit of the One who raised Jesus from the dead
dwells in you, He who raised Christ from the dead will
also give life to your mortal bodies through His Spirit
who indwells you.

In the original Greek text [of Romans 8:2] it is difficult to discern whether the phrase *in Christ Jesus* modifies *the law of the
Spirit of life* or *has freed me*. Actually, the law of the Spirit of life
and the freeing are both in Christ Jesus. Only in Christ Jesus is
there such a law and such a freeing. We may also say that *in
Christ Jesus* modifies *life*. The divine life is in Christ Jesus
(cf. John 1:4; 1 John 5:12). (*The All-inclusive Indwelling Spirit*, p. 26)

Today's Reading

God's desire is that we live as human beings by the divine
life. Many Christians...think that we need to improve ourselves, and because we cannot make it, we need to seek God's
help through prayer....God does not want us to live as angels
or perfect human beings but to live as humans by the divine
life. Many Christians misinterpret the words *eternal life* in
the Bible to mean a condition of living eternally in a physical
paradise. However, eternal life is actually the divine life of
God....Romans 8 reveals that the divine life that is in Christ
Jesus is now being transmitted and transfused into us.

Perhaps some are still not clear about the difference between being virtuous by the human life and living by the divine
life. Life is abstract, but it can be discerned by its manifestations.
Whatever we are able to do by our human life makes us proud,
and pride kills others spiritually. Even if we are quite virtuous,
as long as we are proud, we cannot build, minister life, or supply
anything of the Lord to others. If a brother and his wife are
taught to love and submit to one another, they may accept the

teaching and pray for the Lord to help them to obey the teaching. However, if they are successful by their own self-effort, they will become proud and self-exalted. When we touch them, we will sense not that we are meeting God but that we are meeting proud, self-exalted people. This is the manifestation of being virtuous by our human life. On the other hand, the husband and wife may realize that they cannot love and submit to one another by their own life and that God actually wants them to live a human life as a husband and wife by the divine life. As a result, they may pray, humble themselves, deny their human ability and energy, and live not by themselves but by the Lord as the indwelling Spirit. Then spontaneously, unconsciously, and unintentionally they will love and submit to one another, yet they will not realize that they are being virtuous. Instead, they will feel that they are short in living Christ and expressing His excellent virtues. When we contact such ones, we sense that they are full of Christ. Even if they do not say anything to us, what they are will minister life to us. When we contact such ones, we are nourished, strengthened, edified, and built up. Furthermore, we are spontaneously influenced to live the same kind of life, expressing excellent virtues as human beings living by the divine life, which is in Christ Jesus and is imparted into us by the all-inclusive indwelling Spirit.

In the divine life there is a law that controls us as we live the Christian life. If we live according to this law, we will live a genuine, normal Christian life. Regrettably, most of us live a somewhat abnormal Christian life, because our Christian life is under the control of something else, such as our habit, nature, or culture....We must be controlled and directed by the law of the Spirit of life to experience a genuine and normal Christian life. Romans 8 is a practical and crucial chapter because it reveals the law of the Spirit of life. (*The All-inclusive Indwelling Spirit,* pp. 28-30, 40-41)

Further Reading: The All-inclusive Indwelling Spirit, chs. 3, 5

Enlightenment and inspiration: _____

_____

_____

_____

Morning Nourishment

Rom.
8:4-6

That the righteous requirement of the law might be fulfilled in us, who do not walk according to the flesh but according to the spirit. For those who are according to the flesh mind the things of the flesh; but those who are according to the spirit, the things of the Spirit. For the mind set on the flesh is death, but the mind set on the spirit is life and peace.

Within us there are two substances: flesh and spirit [Rom. 8:4]. We must choose to walk according to the flesh or according to the spirit. It is entirely up to us to make this choice. It is difficult to know what is the spirit, but it is easy to know what is the flesh. In every environment and situation we all can recognize the flesh. When we deduct the flesh, what remains is the spirit. Since we know what is the flesh, we can walk according to the spirit simply by not walking according to the flesh.

We may think that some things are neutral and that it is not possible to know whether or not they are the flesh. However, according to the Bible, there is no third choice or neutral ground; everything is either according to the flesh or the spirit (vv. 4, 6, 9; John 3:6; Gal. 5:17; 6:8; 1 Pet. 3:18). For instance, a wife may prefer to open the window, and her husband may prefer to close it. The window being open or closed may be neutral, but for either spouse to insist on his or her preference is the flesh. If we insist on anything for our own sake, interest, or profit, even if the thing itself is not sinful or immoral, we are walking according to the flesh....As long as we are not walking according to the flesh, we must be walking according to the spirit. (*The All-inclusive Indwelling Spirit,* p. 33)

Today's Reading

The verb in Romans 8:4 is *walk,* but the verb in verse 5 is *are.* Being according to the flesh or the spirit implies more than walking according to the flesh or the spirit. We need to not only *walk* according to the spirit but also constantly *be* according to the spirit, not according to the flesh.

A living according to the spirit and not according to the flesh is the realization of an inward law—the law of the Spirit of life (v. 2). The law of gravity keeps us on the ground....However, if we are in an airplane, another law, the law of aerodynamics, is applied to us to keep us off the ground....If we want to remain on the ground, we need only to stay away from the airplane. However, to remain in the air does not require a great effort. Instead, we must only enter into an airplane. If we are in an airplane, it can overcome the power of gravity to lift us off the ground. Being according to the flesh is like remaining on the ground, and being according to the spirit is like being in an airplane. The law of the Spirit of life in our mingled spirit has the power to overcome the law of sin and of death in our flesh....If we choose to be according to the spirit, the law of the Spirit of life will spontaneously free us from the law of sin and of death. The law of the Spirit of life does not need our help, but it needs our consent. We do not need to do anything to free ourselves from the law of sin and of death. We only need to be according to the spirit.

From the moment we wake up...we should exercise our spirit by calling on the Lord and worshipping, thanking, praising, and exalting Him. Doing this will drive away all the dark thoughts and gird our spirit to guard our entire being. If we practice this, we will not be loose, natural, or short-tempered, because our spirit will be on the alert.

If we exercise our spirit from the very beginning of the day, we will live this way all day long. As a result, when we exercise and release our spirit in the meetings, it will not be a performance but a continuation of our normal daily practice. If we practice this every day, after a few months we will have built up a spiritual habit....We need to live a daily life with a spiritual habit to continually exercise and release our spirit so that we become a person who walks according to the spirit and is according to the spirit. (*The All-inclusive Indwelling Spirit,* pp. 33-34, 67-68)

Further Reading: The All-inclusive Indwelling Spirit, ch. 4

Enlightenment and inspiration: _____

_____

_____

_____

Morning Nourishment

Rom. **For as many as are led by the Spirit of God, these**
8:14-15 **are sons of God. For you have not received a spirit**
of slavery *bringing you* into fear again, but you
have received a spirit of sonship in which we cry,
Abba, Father!

Paul wrote Romans 8 not only according to his revelation but also fully according to his experience. According to
verse 5, we need to mind the things of the Spirit. To mind the
things of the Spirit is to set our mind on the things of the
Spirit....The things of the Spirit of God [1 Cor. 2:14] are the
deep things of God (vv. 10-11) concerning Christ as our portion
(1:2, 9). No one was born, raised, or educated to have a habit of
setting the mind on the Spirit. However, the Bible teaches us
to habitually and continually set our mind not on the things of
the flesh but on the things of the Spirit. We need to build up
such a habit....We need to exercise to keep our mind occupied
by the things concerning Christ not only in the meetings but
also in our daily life, family life, marriage life, school life, and
job life....We must continually have our mind occupied with
the things of the Spirit, the things concerning Christ. (*The All-
inclusive Indwelling Spirit,* pp. 34-35)

Today's Reading

The two spirits, the divine Spirit with our human spirit,
connect all the things concerning Christ to our mind. As long as
our mind is connected to the things concerning Christ by the
two spirits, we are victorious. Our mind represents our entire
being....The secret of spiritual warfare is to not allow our mind
to be vacant. It is especially dangerous to let our mind be
vacant in the morning and when we are resting. When we are
busy with school or work, those things occupy our mind. When
we try to rest, our mind may become vacant, and evil things
may come in. Therefore, especially when we are not busy, we
need to exercise to fill our mind with the things of the Spirit,
the things concerning the glorious Christ. This is our victory.

Romans 8:13 says, "If you live according to the flesh, you must die, but if by the Spirit you put to death the practices of the body, you will live." According to my experience, verse 13 is a direct continuation of verse 5. If we set our mind on the things concerning Christ, we immediately put to death all the practices of our body. After we rise up in the morning, we quickly begin to consider many things that we intend to do. More than nine out of ten things that we intend to do are of the flesh. Therefore, we need a lot of putting to death....If we consider our basic intentions, we will discover that nearly every practice of our body needs to be put to death. The practices of the body are mainly our habits. We need to put to death [by the Spirit] not only our bad habits but also our good habits.

We may wonder how we can live after so much putting to death. Actually, the more we put to death, the more we live. ...Our putting to death the practices of our body by the Spirit is the leading of the Spirit of God [v. 14]. After the putting to death, we know what the Spirit wants us to do, and we have the clear leading. When we feel that we do not know what to do, it is because we are not putting to death the practices of our body by the Spirit....The experiences in verses 13 and 14 eventually lead us to cry, "Abba, Father!" [v. 15].

Now we have seen the way to live by the divine life. First, we need to declare that we choose to be not according to the flesh but according to the spirit (vv. 2, 4). Second, we need to continually set our mind on the things concerning Christ (v. 5). Third, we must put to death the practices of the body by the Spirit (v. 13). Then spontaneously, we will cry, "Abba, Father! Father, I have put to death everything but You. So I cry to You, Abba, Father!" If we practice these things, we are living by the divine life. (*The All-inclusive Indwelling Spirit,* pp. 35-37)

Further Reading: The All-inclusive Indwelling Spirit, ch. 8

Enlightenment and inspiration: _____

_____

_____

_____

Morning Nourishment

Rom. And we know that all things work together for good
8:28-30 to those who love God, to those who are called according to *His* purpose. Because those whom He
foreknew, He also predestinated *to be* conformed to
the image of His Son, that He might be the Firstborn
among many brothers; and those whom He predestinated, these He also called; and those whom He
called, these He also justified; and those whom He justified, these He also glorified.

Romans 8 is the center, the focus, of the Bible and of the
entire universe. Thus, if we are experiencing Romans 8, we
are in the center of the universe. Romans 8 reveals that the
Spirit of life, the law of the Spirit of life, the Spirit of God,
the Spirit of Christ, and the Spirit of the resurrecting One are
all one in the Spirit, who is life to our spirit, mind, and
body. Nothing is more precious than these aspects of the all-
inclusive Spirit, which meet our every need and completely
satisfy us. (*The All-inclusive Indwelling Spirit,* p. 17)

Today's Reading

Romans 8 is mysterious and abstract, yet it is a crucial chapter in the Bible, for it reveals the focal point of God's economy.
The highlight of God's salvation is that He wants to be one with
His redeemed people. God's desire to be one with man is not acci-
dental or temporary but eternal. Ephesians 1:3-5...reveal[s]
that in eternity past God had a heart's desire and purposed to
fulfill this desire. In order to fulfill His desire, God planned to
work Himself into a group of human beings. In other words, in
eternity past God purposed to enter into His redeemed people so
that He could be their life and so that they could be His corporate expression. This is the focus of God's economy.

According to God's purpose, He created the heavens, the
earth, and millions of items with human beings as the center.
Man is the center of God's creation because God's intention is to
be expressed through man. Man can become God's expression

only by God entering into man to be man's life and content and to make man one with Him so that man may live by Him and even live Him out. In this way God is expressed from within man.

The heavens are for the earth, the earth is for man, and God created man with a spirit so that man can receive God [Zech. 12:1]. The crucial part in a transistor radio is the receiver, which receives the radio waves from the air. Without a receiver, a radio does not work. Although there are many radio waves in the air, only a radio with a receiver can substantiate the radio waves. God created man with a spirit as such a receiver to substantiate and receive God.

We human beings are different from animals because we have a spirit as a wonderful receiver....Animals have no thought about God, but throughout history and regardless of race, people have always worshipped. Although what they worship may be wrong, their desire to worship is right. Atheists say that there is no God, yet deep in their being is a desire to worship something. Within man there is a subconscious need to worship God, because man has a spirit. Just as we hunger for food because we have a stomach, we hunger for God because He created a spirit in us.

The Lord said, "God is Spirit, and those who worship Him must worship in spirit and truthfulness" (John 4:24)....We should not try to physically feel, see, smell, or hear God. We must use the proper organ. Just as we must exercise our ears to substantiate sound, we must exercise our spirit to substantiate God....God is real, but we need to exercise the proper organ—our human spirit—to know Him. People often come to a point in their lives when it seems that nothing can satisfy them. Although we may have a good family, education, job, and financial situation, we will come to a point when we realize that there is still a hunger and thirst within that is not satisfied. This hunger and thirst are in our spirit. Man was created with a spirit to seek after God. (*The All-inclusive Indwelling Spirit,* pp. 55-56)

Further Reading: The All-inclusive Indwelling Spirit, ch. 7

Enlightenment and inspiration: _____
_____
_____
_____

Morning Nourishment

Rom. **But you are not in the flesh, but in the spirit, if**
8:9 **indeed the Spirit of God dwells in you. Yet if anyone**
does not have the Spirit of Christ, he is not of Him.
11 **And if the Spirit of the One who raised Jesus from**
the dead dwells in you, He who raised Christ
from the dead will also give life to your mortal
bodies through His Spirit who indwells you.

Although the Bible is composed of sixty-six books and over a
thousand chapters, it has a central thought—Christ as the
embodiment of God wants us to receive Him and give Him the
permission to make His home in our hearts, to dwell in us perma-
nently and eternally. The Triune God created the heavens and
the earth, was incarnated, lived as a man on the earth for thirty-
three and a half years, and died on the cross to accomplish
redemption, take away our sins, and terminate our old man and
the entire old creation. Then He entered into resurrection and
ascension. The central focus in the universe is that this processed
Triune God has come into us and now dwells in us. This is the
greatest miracle. Nothing else in the universe could be more
important than this. (*The All-inclusive Indwelling Spirit*, p. 49)

Today's Reading

We need to see that the indwelling of the processed Triune
God is not a mere theory or doctrine but a real and present
fact....If we see that the Triune God lives in us, we will be
ecstatic....We should all be full of joy since the Triune God is
indwelling us and is one with us. He is our life and our person,
and He is making us His home. It is crucial that we recognize
this fact. We need to pray, "O Lord Jesus, show us this glorious
fact." We need His mercy to see a vision that the processed
Triune God, who has accomplished everything and is now the
all-inclusive life-giving Spirit, dwells in us. Even if we see only
a little, it is better than nothing. Although we may not be
ecstatic, as long as we are happy, it is good enough. A Christian
must be a happy person. The Christian life is a happy life.

We need to see that the indwelling Spirit is the Triune God. According to the New Testament Greek, in the expression *the Spirit of God,* the Spirit and God are in apposition, indicating that the Spirit and God are one (Rom. 8:9). Similarly, *the Spirit of Christ, the Spirit of the resurrecting One,* and *the Spirit of life* in Romans 8 indicate that the Spirit is Christ, the resurrecting One, and life (vv. 9, 11, 2). Therefore, since the Spirit indwells us, all three of the Triune God are in us as life. Actually, the three of the Triune God are all one. In John 14:23 the Lord said clearly that if we love Him, He and the Father will come and make an abode with us....Wherever one of the Godhead is, the other two are as well, because the three of the Godhead not only coexist but also coinhere. This is a mystery. To coexist is to exist simultaneously, and to coinhere is to exist within one another.

In Romans 8 the indwelling Spirit is called the Spirit of God, the Spirit of Christ, and the Spirit of the resurrecting One. Thus, we can say that the Spirit in Romans 8 is the all-inclusive Spirit as the ultimate consummation and application of the Triune God. The Spirit is the link of the Triune God to us, for when He is present, the Triune God is present....God may seem far away and objective to some, but the Spirit is always subjective. The Spirit is the reaching, the application, of God to us. The current of electricity is the application and reaching of electricity from a distant power plant to a building. When electricity is thus applied as a current, it becomes subjective. Similarly, the Spirit is the application and the reaching of the Triune God to us.

The Triune God as the all-inclusive Spirit is within us for us to experience and enjoy by taking Him as our life and our person....Within every genuine believer of Christ, there are two persons: the believer and the Triune God. We are the container of the Triune God, and He is within us as our life and our person. (*The All-inclusive Indwelling Spirit,* pp. 49-51)

Further Reading: The All-inclusive Indwelling Spirit, ch. 1

Enlightenment and inspiration: _____

_____

_____

_____

Morning Nourishment

Rom. **If Christ is in you, though the body is dead because**
8:10 **of sin, the spirit is life because of righteousness.**
  6 **...The mind set on the spirit is life and peace.**
 11 **...If the Spirit of the One who raised Jesus from the**
       dead dwells in you, He who raised Christ from
       the dead will also give life to your mortal bodies
       through His Spirit who indwells you.

When Christ enters into us, our spirit is regenerated. Thus, our spirit is life (Rom. 8:10). When we love the Lord and set our mind on the things concerning Him, our mind is life (v. 6). Furthermore, if the Spirit of the resurrecting One indwells us, He will give life to our body (v. 11). For the Spirit to indwell us, we must give Him the permission to settle within us and saturate our inner being.

We need to realize that according to God's economy and eternal purpose, what God wants to do in His salvation is to work Himself into us, His redeemed people, as our life. God's desire to work Himself into us as our life is the focus of the Bible....The forgiveness of sins and salvation from hell are great and necessary parts of God's salvation, yet they are not the central concern of God's salvation. The central focus of God's salvation is God working Himself into us as our life. (*The All-inclusive Indwelling Spirit,* pp. 51-52, 63-64)

Today's Reading

The life that is given to our spirit, mind, and body is the Spirit, who is the consummation of the Triune God. Life, the Triune God, and Christ are one in the Spirit. Therefore, as we continually breathe in the Spirit as life and allow Him to spread into all our being, more and more of Christ is added into us. We become different when Christ as the life-giving Spirit is added into us, because we receive a new element. This is to know God in the experiential way of life. It is more than believing and trusting in an objective God and more than merely receiving gifts or power from God for our use or strength. Instead, it is to possess, experience, and enjoy the subjective God within our being.

When God is thus repeatedly added into our being, we will receive the life element that causes us to grow....Growth requires the addition of a new element....We need more than the knowledge of an objective God in our mind; we need to have the element of the subjective God added into our being. This occurs not by teaching but by experiencing. Therefore, whenever we feel weak in our spirit, mind, or body toward the things of God, we need to call on the name of the Lord....To call on the name of the Lord is to breathe life into us, and this life is nothing less than Christ as the embodiment of God realized as the Spirit....In this way, the divine element is added into our being, and we grow with this element. As a result, our Christian life and growth will be normal and healthy.

In the divine life is a law, which is the working, the function, of this life (Rom. 8:2). While we are growing with the element of the divine life, this life has an automatic function, the law of life. This law regulates us from within, shaping us into the form of Christ. Thus, we are being conformed to the image of Christ and will eventually be exactly the same as He is (v. 29). This is not ethics, religion, or improvement of character; much less is it something of habit, nature, or culture. Instead, it is the Triune God indwelling us so that we can take Him as our life, our life supply, and even our person and thereby live by the divine life and grow with the divine element every day. While we are growing with this life element, the law of life works in us automatically to shape us, conform us, into the image of Christ. The Body of Christ, the fullness of Christ, the new man, and the mutual habitation of God and man issue from our experience of this life. Ultimately, this life will prepare the bride of Christ, which will cause the Lord to come back and usher us into the next age. For this reason, the crucial focus of the Bible and the universe is in Romans 8. (*The All-inclusive Indwelling Spirit*, pp. 53-54)

Further Reading: The All-inclusive Indwelling Spirit, ch. 6

Enlightenment and inspiration: _____

_____

_____

_____

Hymns, #73

1   Glorious, mighty Name of Jesus,
      Into Thy dear Name I flee;
    "Set aloft," I praise and worship,
      For Thy Name is victory!

2   Blessed Jesus! Mighty Savior!
      In Thy Name is all I need;
    Just to breathe the Name of Jesus,
      Is to drink of Life indeed.

3   Glorious, mighty Name of Jesus,
      Heav'n and earth its pow'r proclaim;
    But forgiven sinners only,
      Know the balm of Jesus' Name.

4   Jesus! Jesus! Name most precious,
      Balm in pain or mighty sword;
    In Thy Name, we live and conquer,
      Blessed, glorious, coming Lord.

Composition for prophecy with main point and sub-points: _____

_____
_____
_____
_____
_____
_____
_____
_____
_____
_____
_____
_____
_____
_____
_____
_____
_____
_____
_____
_____
_____
_____
_____
_____
_____
_____
_____
_____
_____
_____
_____
_____
_____
_____
_____
_____

The Focus of God's Economy— the Mingled Spirit

Scripture Reading: 1 Cor. 6:17; Rom. 8:4, 16; Eph. 1:17; 2:22; 4:23

Day 1

I. The focus of God's economy is the mingled spirit, the divine Spirit mingled with the human spirit; whatever God intends to do or accomplish is related to this focus (Eph. 3:9, 5; 1:17; 2:22; 4:23; 5:18; 6:18):

    A. The union of God and man is a union of the two spirits, the Spirit of God and the spirit of man; the union of these two spirits is the deepest mystery in the Bible (1 Cor. 2:11-14; Eph. 5:32).

    B. The essence of the New Testament is the two spirits—the divine Spirit and the human spirit—mingled together as one spirit (1 Cor. 6:17):

        1. The word *joined* in 1 Corinthians 6:17 refers to the believers' organic union with the Lord through believing into Him (John 3:15-16; 15:4-5).

        2. The spirit in 1 Corinthians 6:17 is both the Spirit of the Lord and our spirit (15:45b; 2 Cor. 3:17; Rom. 8:16).

        3. The expression *one spirit* indicates the mingling of the Lord as the Spirit with our spirit (1 Cor. 6:17).

Day 2

        4. The implications of 1 Corinthians 6:17 are marvelous and far-reaching:

           a. This verse reveals that we and Christ are one wonderful, living entity.

           b. To be one spirit with the Lord implies that we are in Him and that He is in us and that we and He are one in life (John 14:20; 15:4-5).

    C. The mingled spirit is a spirit that is one spirit with God and that is the same as God in His life and nature but not in His Godhead (1 John 5:11; 2 Pet. 1:4).

D. The divine Spirit and the human spirit are mingled as one within us so that we can live the life of a God-man, a life that is God yet man and man yet God (Gal. 2:20; Phil. 1:19-21a).

E. The God-man living is the living of the two spirits, the Spirit of God and the spirit of man joined and mingled together as one (Gal. 2:20; Rom. 8:4).

Day 3

F. To be proper Christians, we must know that the Lord Jesus today as the embodiment of the Triune God is the Spirit indwelling our spirit and mingled with our spirit as one spirit (2 Cor. 3:17; 1 Cor. 15:45b; 6:17).

II. **All our spiritual experiences, such as our fellowship with the Lord, our prayer to Him, and our living with Him, are in this mingled spirit (John 4:24; 15:4-5; Rom. 1:9; 8:4, 16; Eph. 1:17; 2:22; 4:23; 6:18; Phil. 2:1):**

A. Romans 8 speaks of the Spirit of life, the spirit of the believers, and the mingled spirit (vv. 2, 9, 11, 15-16):

1. Through the Spirit of life the eternal, only wise God, according to the revelation of the mystery hidden through the ages, dispenses Himself in His processed and consummated Spirit into the believers to be their consummated salvation as their life and everything (16:25; 8:11; 5:10).

2. Through the regenerated human spirit the believers participate in God's dynamic salvation as their living (8:10, 16).

3. "The Spirit...with our spirit" (v. 16) is the most crucial secret in Romans for God to execute His dynamic salvation and for the believers to participate in it.

4. We need to know these two spirits in the divine enlightenment so that, by the Spirit of life mingled with our regenerated spirit, we may enter into the intrinsic significance of the dynamic salvation of God in Christ,

which is the Triune God processed and consummated to be our eternal inheritance for
our enjoyment (vv. 2, 10, 16; 2 Cor. 13:14; Acts
26:18; Eph. 1:13-14).

Day 4   B. The spirit of faith in 2 Corinthians 4:13 is the mingled spirit—the Holy Spirit mingled with the
regenerated human spirit:
1. Faith is in our spirit, which is mingled with
the Holy Spirit (1:24; 5:7).
2. We must exercise the spirit of faith to believe
and to speak the things that we have experienced of the Lord, especially His death and
resurrection (4:13).
3. It is by the mingled spirit as the spirit of faith
that the apostles lived a crucified life in resurrection for the carrying out of their ministry (3:8-9; 4:1, 10-12; 5:18).

C. To abide in the Lord as the true vine is to be one
spirit with Him and to live in the mingled spirit
(John 15:1, 4-5; 1 Cor. 6:17):
1. The Christian life is a life of abiding in the
Lord as the true vine (John 15:1, 4-5; 1 John
2:24, 27-28; cf. 4:1).
2. The mutual abiding in John 15:4-5 is the
practice of being one spirit with the Lord.

Day 5   D. Ultimately, the Bible requires only one thing of
us—that we walk according to the mingled spirit
(Rom. 8:4):
1. The key to experiencing and enjoying the
processed and consummated Triune God
through the divine dispensing is found in
the wonderful Spirit who is in our regenerated spirit and who has become one spirit
with our spirit (Phil. 1:19; 1 Cor. 15:45b;
6:17).
2. By living in the mingled spirit, we can experience Christ as everything to us (1:2, 9, 24, 30;
2:8, 10; 3:11; 5:7-8; 10:3-4; 11:3; 12:12; 15:20,
45b, 47).

3. When we live in the mingled spirit, we spontaneously bear the cross (Rom. 8:4; 1 Cor. 6:17; Matt. 16:24).

4. Whether or not we are under Satan's authority is not determined by the things we do but is determined by whether we are in the spirit or in the flesh; if we remain in the mingled spirit, we will be kept from Satan, and the evil one will have no way to touch us (Gal. 5:16-17; 1 John 5:4, 18-21).

Day 6

5. To live in the spirit is to let Christ fill and saturate us until He permeates our whole being and is thereby expressed through us (Eph. 3:16-20).

E. By living, walking, and having our being in the mingled spirit, we will be saved in life to the extent that God and we, we and God, will be completely mingled as one, having one life and one living (Gal. 2:20; Phil. 1:19-21a).

F. If we enter experientially into the depths of the truth concerning the mingled spirit, our inner being will be radically changed, and our life, ministry, and service in the church will be affected in a revolutionary way (1 Cor. 6:17; Rom. 8:4).

Morning Nourishment

Rom. **The Spirit Himself witnesses with our spirit that**
8:16 **we are children of God.**
1 Cor. **But he who is joined to the Lord is one spirit.**
6:17

The divine Spirit is in our human spirit. Romans 8:16 says that the Spirit witnesses with our spirit, that we are the children of God. Furthermore, 1 Corinthians 6:17 says that he who is joined to the Lord is one spirit. Now we have not only the divine Spirit in our spirit but also the mingling of the divine Spirit with our spirit. Thus, the two spirits are one.... Praise the Lord that these two spirits have been mingled into one spirit! This is the reason that in the verses concerning our walk in the spirit, it is difficult for the translators to determine whether to render *pneuma* as "Spirit" or as "spirit." Actually, to walk according to the Spirit means to walk according to both the divine Spirit and the human spirit, according to the two spirits mingled as one. The two spirits are mingled not in the heavens nor outside of us but within us. This is the focus of the divine economy. Whatever God intends to do or accomplish is related to this focus. If we would have certain basic spiritual experiences, we must have a clear understanding that the focus of God's economy is the mingled spirit, the divine Spirit mingled with the human spirit. (*Basic Training,* p. 55)

Today's Reading

We will consider the union of the Spirit of God and the spirit of the believers....We have used this term *union* quite much, but concerning the union of God and man, we do not have adequate knowledge. The union of God and man is altogether a matter of the union of the two spirits, the Spirit of God and the spirit of man. God is Spirit and man has a spirit; thus, these two spirits can be united together as one. But how does the union of these two spirits occur? This is the deepest mystery in the Bible, and it is difficult for man to comprehend. (*The Issue of the Union of the Consummated Spirit of the Triune God and the Regenerated Spirit of the Believers,* p. 34)

Within every substance there is an essence, the essential constituent of the substance. An apple is substantial, but within this substance there is the apple juice as its essence. It is easy for many readers of the Bible to understand the story of Jesus. However, it is not as easy to see the extract of what the New Testament speaks concerning Jesus. The history of Jesus is the substance of the New Testament, but we need to see the essence of this substance. Some people have obtained doctoral degrees in the study of the Bible, but they may have seen only the substance. They can tell you what is taught in the four Gospels, in the Acts, in the Epistles of Paul, James, Peter, John, and Jude, and in Revelation. They have seen the substance of the New Testament, but very few Bible readers have seen the essence within the New Testament. If we see the essence of the New Testament, we will rejoice. The essence of the New Testament is the mingling of the divine Spirit with our human spirit. These two spirits are mingled as one (1 Cor. 6:17). (*The Experience and Growth in Life,* p. 131)

The word *joined* in [1 Corinthians 6:17] refers to the believers' organic union with the Lord through believing into Him (John 3:15-16). This union is illustrated by that of the branches with the vine (John 15:4-5). It is a matter not only of life, but also in life, the divine life. Such a union with the resurrected Lord can only be in our spirit.

The expression "one spirit" indicates the mingling of the Lord as the Spirit with our spirit. Our spirit has been regenerated by the Spirit of God (John 3:6), who is now in us (1 Cor. 6:19) and is one with our spirit (Rom. 8:16). This is the realization of the Lord who became the life-giving Spirit through resurrection (1 Cor. 15:45; 2 Cor. 3:17), and who is now with our spirit (2 Tim. 4:22). This mingled spirit is often referred to in Paul's Epistles, as in Romans 8:4-6. (*Life-study of 1 Corinthians,* pp. 345-346)

Further Reading: Basic Training, msg. 5; *The Issue of the Union of the Consummated Spirit of the Triune God and the Regenerated Spirit of the Believers,* chs. 1-3

Enlightenment and inspiration: _____

_____

_____

_____

Morning Nourishment

John In that day you will know that I am in My Father,
14:20 and you in Me, and I in you.

Phil. For I know that for me this will turn out to salvation
1:19 through your petition and *the* bountiful supply of
      the Spirit of Jesus Christ.

21 For to me, to live is Christ...

One of the greatest verses in the Bible, 1 Corinthians 6:17, says, "He who is joined to the Lord is one spirit." The implications of this verse are marvelous and far-reaching. We, the believers, are one spirit with the Lord. How tremendous! This implies that we are in Him and that He is in us. It also implies that we and He have been mingled, blended organically, to become one in life. To be one spirit with the Lord implies that we and He are a living entity....To say that we are one spirit with the Lord...certainly does imply the mingling of divinity with humanity. In the words of #501 in *Hymns,* "God mingled with humanity lives in me my all to be." To be one spirit with the Lord means that we are blended with Him organically and mingled with Him in life. We urgently need more experience of this. We need to remain rooted in Christ and absorb all that He is into us. Then we and He, He and we, will be blended together in life organically to be one spirit. How profound! How wonderful! (*Life-study of Colossians,* pp. 457-458)

Today's Reading

When we are one spirit with the Lord, we cannot be affected by anything negative. Sin, the world, Satan, and Hades have nothing to do with us, for we are one spirit with the Triune God. This should not merely be a doctrine. In our experience this must be living and organic. Our spiritual being, our inner man, the regenerated spirit, must be permeated with the Lord and mingled with Him to form a single, living entity. This will result in growth and building. (*Life-study of Colossians,* p. 458)

Our spirit was created by God but became dead through the fall. But later it was regenerated by God. Not only so, after regeneration the regenerating Spirit remains in our regenerated spirit and mingles Himself with our spirit to make the two one. Not only are we God-men but also we are one with God, one spirit with God. The human spirit and the divine Spirit are not only joined and mingled but are also one spirit. The Spirit is life and the One who gives life. God is the Spirit and in His marvelous organic salvation, He has made us one spirit with Him. This is just a simple word in 1 Corinthians 6:17, but I never saw this truth until after I had studied the Bible for at least thirty years. One day I realized that I am one spirit with God. This is not a small thing. Regretfully, even in the Lord's recovery, many of the elders and even the co-workers do not know their real status. Our real status is that we are one spirit with God. We have been saved to such a high level. What God is, we are.

According to 1 Corinthians 6:17 God's intention in His organic salvation is to join the believer's spirit with His Spirit as one spirit—a mingled spirit. Eventually, this is not just the mingled spirit but a spirit that is one spirit with God, that is the same as God in His life and nature but not in His Godhead. (*The Divine and Mystical Realm,* pp. 53-54)

The regenerated spirit of the believers and the consummated Spirit of God are mingled as one spirit (1 Cor. 6:17). Thus, the Spirit of God is no longer like a single hand that cannot produce clapping sounds; rather, the two spirits can "clap" together. Today, the Spirit of God and the human spirit are mingled as one within us so that we can live a God-man life, a life that is God yet man and man yet God. Hence, the God-man life is a living of the two spirits, the Spirit of God and the spirit of man joined and mingled together as one. (*The Issue of the Union of the Consummated Spirit of the Triune God and the Regenerated Spirit of the Believers,* p. 30)

Further Reading: The Divine and Mystical Realm, ch. 4; *The Two Spirits in Romans,* chs. 1, 7

Enlightenment and inspiration: blended together

Morning Nourishment

Rom. But you are not in the flesh, but in the spirit, if
8:9 indeed the Spirit of God dwells in you. Yet if
anyone does not have the Spirit of Christ, he is not
of Him.

11 And if the Spirit of the One who raised Jesus from
the dead dwells in you, He who raised Christ from
the dead will also give life to your mortal bodies
through His Spirit who indwells you.

We all must realize that the most crucial part of our being
is our spirit. Many times our fellowship and contact with the
saints help us to realize that we are still in our flesh and our
soul—our mind, emotion, and will. We have to learn to always
live not in our flesh or in our soul but in our spirit. When we
are angry with someone, we are often in our flesh. Then when
we realize that we should be nice to them, we act like gentle-
men and talk very thoughtfully with much logic. This is to
talk, live, and behave ourselves in the soul. Neither living in
the flesh nor living in the soul count before God....We should
be spiritual, walking in our spirit (1 Cor. 2:11-13, 15). To be
proper Christians, we must know that the Lord Jesus today as
the embodiment of the Triune God is the Spirit (2 Cor. 3:17)
indwelling our spirit and mingled with our spirit as one spirit
(1 Cor. 6:17). (*Messages to the Trainees in Fall 1990*, pp. 67-68)

Today's Reading

God Himself, Christ, and even we human beings are mysterious. We do not even know ourselves. We must simply
believe that God created us with a human spirit. Moreover,
God is Spirit, and He became incarnated, putting on flesh and
blood. Then He died, was buried, and in His resurrection He
became the life-giving Spirit. When we believed in Him, He
entered into our spirit as the life-giving Spirit. Now the Spirit
works together with our spirit, and the two spirits have
become one to such an extent that it is difficult to discern

which is which. If we do not know our spirit, we cannot live a proper Christian life. The Christian life is altogether a life in our mingled spirit [1 Cor. 6:17]. (*Messages to the Trainees in Fall 1990,* pp. 68-69)

The divine Spirit of life is the Spirit of God processed and consummated to be the life-giving, compounded, and indwelling Spirit, who indwells the believers as the reality of the pneumatic, pneumatized Christ, as the consummation of the processed and consummated Triune God, and as the reality of the divine resurrection. It is through such a Spirit of life that the eternal, only wise God, according to the revelation of the mystery hidden through the ages (Rom. 16:25), dispenses Himself in His processed and consummated Trinity into the believers to be their dynamic salvation as their life and everything.

The human spirit of the believers is the believers' spirit regenerated and indwelt by the divine Spirit of life and mingled with the divine Spirit of life as one spirit. It is through such a human spirit that the people chosen by God participate in the dynamic salvation of God as their living in this age and their destiny in eternity. Hence, "the Spirit...with our spirit" in verse 16 of Romans 8 (the key chapter of the book of Romans concerning the Spirit of life and the spirit of the believers) is the most crucial secret in the whole book of Romans for God to execute His dynamic salvation and for the believers to participate in it. We all have to know these two spirits in the divine enlightenment that we may enter, by the Spirit of life in our regenerated spirit which is mingled with the Spirit of life, into the intrinsic essence of the dynamic salvation of God in Christ, which is the Triune God processed and consummated to be our eternal inheritance for our enjoyment. (*Crystallization-study of the Epistle to the Romans,* pp. 174-175)

Further Reading: Messages to the Trainees in Fall 1990, chs. 7-9

Enlightenment and inspiration: _____

_____

_____

_____

Morning Nourishment

2 Cor. And having the same spirit of faith according to that
4:13 which is written, "I believed, therefore I spoke," we
also believe, therefore we also speak.
John I am the vine; you are the branches. He who abides
15:5 in Me and I in him, he bears much fruit; for apart
from Me you can do nothing.

The spirit [of faith in 2 Corinthians 4:13] is the mingled
spirit, the divine Spirit mingled with the regenerated human
spirit. In their comments on this verse, both Alford and Vincent
spoke concerning the mingled spirit, but their speaking was
somewhat vague. Alford said, "Not distinctly the Holy Spirit,—
but still not merely a human disposition: the indwelling Holy
Spirit penetrates and characterizes the whole renewed man."
On the one hand, Alford speaks of the Holy Spirit. On the other
hand, he indicates that something human, signified by the word
disposition, is also involved. Actually, what Alford was referring
to was the human spirit. Vincent says, "Spirit of faith: not distinctly the Holy Spirit, nor, on the other hand, a human faculty
or disposition, but blending both." Vincent's remarks are an
improvement upon those of Alford. The word faculty is certainly
an improvement over disposition. Furthermore, Vincent speaks
of a blending of the Spirit with a particular human faculty. This
blending is actually the mingling of the Holy Spirit with our
human spirit. (*Life-study of 2 Corinthians,* pp. 302-303)

Today's Reading

Today we have a more clear and definite utterance. We do not
need to use the word disposition or faculty to describe the spirit
of faith in 2 Corinthians 4:13, for we know that this spirit is our
spirit mingled with the Holy Spirit. We must exercise such a
spirit to believe and speak, as the psalmist did (Psa. 116:10), the
things we have experienced of the Lord, especially His death
and resurrection. Faith is in our spirit, which is mingled with the
Holy Spirit, not in our mind. Doubts are in our mind. The
spirit here indicates that it is by the mingled spirit that the

apostles lived a crucified life in resurrection for carrying out
their ministry. (*Life-study of 2 Corinthians,* p. 303)

God is Spirit for man to contact Him and receive Him into
man, and man has a spirit for man to contact God and contain
God that God and man may have an organic union (John 4:24;
1 John 4:13; 2 Tim. 4:22a; 1 Cor. 6:17). If God were not the
Spirit, He could not contact us, and we could not contact Him. God
the Father is the source; God the Son is the course; and God the
Spirit is the flow to reach us (2 Cor. 13:14). Thus, the Spirit is
the reaching of the Divine Trinity to man. God reaches us in the
Son as the Spirit. Ephesians 2:18 says, "For through Him we
both have access in one Spirit unto the Father." The Spirit is
the access for us to contact God, receive God, and contain God.

Our union with God is not like the union in today's American
labor unions. That union is in an organizational and coexisting
way, but our union with God is organic. It is a union not only of
coexistence but also of coinherence. Today we are coinhering
with God. He lives in us, and we live in Him. In John 15 the Lord
said, "Abide in Me and I in you" (v. 4a). First John 4:15 and 16
speak of God abiding in us and us in God. This is a mutual abiding, and this mutual abiding is coinherence. It is only after being
regenerated to have God in us as our life and nature that we are
in union with God organically. This union is a coinherence, a
mutual abiding. This is the Bible's revelation concerning God
and man. We all have to know Him and know ourselves to such
an extent. (*The Spirit with Our Spirit,* pp. 15-16)

First, you must know that today your Savior is this Spirit
abiding in you. Second, before you do anything in your daily
living and walk, you must abide in Him. The Lord said that He
will abide in the one who abides in Him. If you abide in Him,
you will enjoy His salvation and all of His riches. (*A Living of
Mutual Abiding with the Lord in Spirit,* p. 47)

*Further Reading: The Spirit with Our Spirit, ch. 1; A Living of
Mutual Abiding with the Lord in Spirit, chs. 2-4*

Enlightenment and inspiration: _____

_____

_____

_____

Morning Nourishment

Rom. **That the righteous requirement of the law might**
8:4 **be fulfilled in us, who do not walk according to the**
flesh but according to the spirit.

1 Cor. **But of Him you are in Christ Jesus, who became**
1:30 **wisdom to us from God: both righteousness and**
sanctification and redemption.

If the Lord is merciful to open your eyes and show you this matter, your entire Christian life will have a great turn. We should all read the Bible again. Ultimately, the entire Bible requires only one thing of us—to walk according to the mingled spirit, which is the all-inclusive Spirit mingled with our regenerated spirit. First Corinthians 6:17 tells us, "He who is joined to the Lord is one spirit." If our disposition is manifested, this proves that we are not in spirit. If we criticize and judge carelessly, this also proves that we are not in spirit....To be in spirit is simply to be in spirit, and to not be in spirit is simply to not be in spirit. We need to see that the reality of all spiritual things is in the spirit. The church itself is in the spirit, the building of the church is in the spirit, and the eternal testimony of the church is in the spirit. This is the hinge, the secret, and the key to our Christian life and our church life. (*Living in the Spirit*, p. 29)

Today's Reading

Whatever God is, is in this Spirit. The Father, the Son, Jesus, Christ, humanity, crucifixion, resurrection, and ascension are all implied in this wonderful Spirit that has been intensified to become the seven Spirits of God. We all need such a full definition of the Spirit. We need to accept the vision of this Spirit found in the Bible and then pray ourselves into the realization of this Spirit.

Because this Spirit is so rich and bountiful, Philippians 1:19 speaks of the bountiful supply of the Spirit of Jesus Christ. The reason the supply of this Spirit is bountiful is that the Spirit includes God, the riches of the Father and the Son, the element of Jesus' humanity, and the element of Christ, the anointed One of God. This Spirit also includes crucifixion, resurrection, and ascension. All this is found in the Spirit. This Spirit is not merely a power, but a person. This wonderful Spirit has been intensified sevenfold to become the seven Spirits of God sent forth into all the earth (Rev. 5:6). Today the very Spirit we have received into us is such a Spirit. May we all have a thorough and rich revelation of this Spirit. (*Basic Training*, pp. 54-55)

The Bible says that we need to live in the spirit. If we have children, we need to live in the spirit, and if we do not have children, we also need to live in the spirit. If our children are obedient, we need to live in the spirit, and if they are disobedient, we still need to live in the spirit. As long as we live in the spirit, we will spontaneously bear the cross. To bear the cross is to deny our self and to give up our own choice. How can we deny our self? How can we allow the Lord to make choices for us? The only way is to live in the spirit.

Do not think that merely being zealous and serving God is sufficient. Saul of Tarsus was also zealous and also served God, yet he was under the authority of Satan. His service to God, his zeal, and his keeping of the law were all under Satan's authority. Can we say that our zeal, our having morning watch, and our endeavoring in doing many things are not under Satan's authority? Whether or not we are under Satan's authority is not determined by the things we do. Rather, it is determined by whether we are in the spirit or in the flesh. Do we have morning watch in our natural being or in our spirit? If we have morning watch in our natural being, then even though we may rise at 5:30 A.M., our morning watch can be utilized by Satan. However, if we have morning watch in the spirit, there will be a different flavor.

We need to turn to our spirit. Being holy, victorious, or freed from sin is not what matters. The only thing that matters is that we live in the spirit where the Lord dwells. (*Living in the Spirit*, pp. 16, 26-27)

Further Reading: Living in the Spirit, chs. 1-2; The Exercise of Our Spirit, ch. 6

Enlightenment and inspiration: _____

_____

_____

_____

Morning Nourishment

Eph. **May be full of strength to apprehend with all the**
3:18-20 **saints what the breadth and length and height and**
depth are and to know the knowledge-surpassing
love of Christ, that you may be filled unto all the
fullness of God. But to Him who is able to do super-
abundantly above all that we ask or think, accord-
ing to the power which operates in us.

The secret of the Christian life is to live in the spirit....To live
in the spirit is not to engage in religious worship, religious service, or religious work. To live in the spirit is to let Christ fill and
saturate us until He permeates our whole being and is thereby
expressed through us. It is not a matter of husbands being able
to love their wives or of wives being able to love their husbands.
Rather, it is a matter of living in the spirit and allowing Christ as
the life-giving Spirit to permeate our entire being and to express
God through us. This is the overcoming life of a Christian, the
family life of a Christian, and the church life of a Christian.
...The reality of the church is to live in the spirit. The spirit that
we are referring to is not merely the Holy Spirit but is our created and regenerated spirit....We need to turn to our spirit and
pay attention to being in our spirit. Most people pay attention to
their minds and their feelings, but very few people pay attention
to being in the spirit. (*Living in the Spirit,* p. 17)

Today's Reading

The highest gospel is not merely concerning the forgiveness
of sins and deliverance from hell that we may receive eternal
blessing. Rather, the highest gospel is that we would be saved to
the extent that God and we, we and God, are completely mingled
as one, having one life and one living. We were fallen sinners—
wicked, degraded, evil, and desolate—yet we can have one life
and one living with God. God can abide with us and live with us.
Do we believe this? If we do believe this, it may be our belief in
theory but not be our living. We may have been Christians for
decades, yet we may have never had the deep realization that

the gospel of God saves us into Him to live with Him so that He and we can have one life and one living....We may have seen the sweetness of the Lord Jesus in His words, acts, and conduct. Nevertheless, regardless of how sweet He is, He is still He, and we are still we. We should read John 15:4, which says, "Abide in Me and I in you." We should read John 6:57, which says, "As the living Father has sent Me and I live because of the Father, so he who eats Me, he also shall live because of Me." These words are much deeper, showing us that the Lord is not only near us but is also mingled with us. (*Living in the Spirit*, p. 32)

The way Paul deals with the problems among the Corinthian believers is not shallow or superficial. On the contrary, it is deep and profound. As Paul deals with the different problems, he brings us back to the central vision of God's economy—to the Triune God as the all-inclusive life-giving Spirit dwelling in our spirit. The Spirit today is the processed Triune God indwelling our whole being....Christians have problems because they lack the experience of the all-inclusive, life-giving indwelling Spirit. For this reason, Paul eventually brings us back to this Spirit in our spirit.

We should not think that 1 Corinthians is a shallow book dealing with problems in the church. Yes, in this book Paul does deal with many problems. But at the same time he brings us into the central vision of God's economy, for he brings us back to the Spirit as the ultimate consummation of the processed Triune God.

If you get into the depths of these verses, your life, ministry, and service in the church will be affected in a revolutionary way. Your inner being and your entire church life will be radically changed. May we all pray about these verses until such a change takes place within us. (*Life-study of 1 Corinthians*, pp. 358-359)

Further Reading: Living in the Spirit, chs. 3-4; The Conclusion of the New Testament, msg. 151

Enlightenment and inspiration: ___pay attentation___
_____
_____
_____

Hymns, #1199

1   God's intention in this universe is with humanity,
    So the Lord became the Spirit just with man to mingled be.
    We rejoice that we can all partake of His economy.
       Yes, mingling is the way.

       Mingle, mingle, hallelujah,
       Mingle, mingle, hallelujah,
       Mingle, mingle, hallelujah,
       Yes, mingling is the way!

2   In the center of our being, past our mind, emotion, will,
    Is a certain spot created to contain the Lord until
    By His flowing and His flooding He will all our being fill;
       Yes, mingling is the way.

3   Now within the Lord's recov'ry, we're so glad to find the way
    To experience the Triune God and live by Him today—
    Get into the mingled spirit, and within the spirit stay;
       Yes, mingling is the way.

4   In the midst of seven lampstands, now the Son of Man we see;
    Eyes ablaze and feet a'burning, He's for God's recovery.
    God's intention He's accomplishing—a corporate entity;
       Yes, mingling is the way.

5   In our daily life and all we are and do and think and say,
    How we need a deeper mingling just to gain the Lord each day;
    Lord, we give ourselves completely just to take the mingled way.
       Yes, mingling is the way.

6   From the fruit of daily living, New Jerusalem we'll see,
    It's the ultimate in mingling—it's divine humanity.
    And what joy that we can share it all, and share it corporately.
       Yes, mingling is the way.

Composition for prophecy with main point and sub-points: _____

_____

_____

_____

_____

_____

_____

_____

_____

_____

_____

_____

_____

_____

_____

_____

_____

_____

_____

_____

_____

_____

_____

_____

_____

_____

_____

_____

_____

_____

_____

Living in the Focus
of the Lord's Recovery as Inoculators
and Ministers of the New Covenant

Scripture Reading: 2 Tim. 2:1-7, 15; 2 Cor. 2:14-16; 3:1-3, 16-18; 4:1, 4-7

Day 1   I. **Second Timothy is a book written for inoculators, those who would inoculate others against the decline of the church (2:1-7, 15):**
   A. The inoculator is a teacher (v. 2; Eph. 3:2):
      1. If someone in a local church has a deposit of the Lord's healthy words, he should train the faithful ones so that they also may have a good deposit from the Lord and be competent to teach others (1 Tim. 6:20; 2 Tim. 1:12-14).
      2. We must shepherd the saints with the teaching of God's economy (Eph. 4:11; cf. 1 Tim. 3:2; 4:11-16):
         a. We should shepherd people by dispensing the divine life in the humanity of Jesus to cherish them and by teaching them the divine truths in the divinity of Christ to nourish them (Eph. 5:29).
         b. Shepherding the flock of God by declaring to them all the counsel of God, the economy of God, protects the church from the destroyers of God's building, mingles them with the Triune God as grace, and binds them together in His oneness (Acts 20:26-30; Eph. 4:14; 1 Tim. 1:3-4; Rom. 16:17; cf. Ezek. 33:1-11; 34:25; Zech. 11:7).
      3. The inoculating teacher, as a good minister of Christ Jesus, is nourished with the words of the faith and exercises his spirit to live Christ in his daily life for the church life (1 Tim. 4:6-7).
Day 2   B. The inoculator is a soldier (2 Tim. 2:3-4):
      1. The apostles considered their ministry a warfare for Christ, just as the priestly service was considered a military service, a warfare (Num. 4:23, 30, 35; 1 Tim. 1:18; 2 Tim. 4:7).

2. The Lord's ministry is the sounding of the trumpet for the army to go to war; to war the good warfare is to war against the different teachings of the dissenters and to carry out God's economy according to the apostle's ministry (1 Cor. 14:8; 1 Tim. 1:18; Num. 10:9; Judg. 7:18).

3. To fight a good fight for the Lord's interests on this earth, we must clear away all earthly entanglements and lay hold on the eternal life, not trusting in our human life (2 Tim. 4:7; 1 Tim. 6:12; cf. 2 Cor. 5:4).

4. We must fight the battle against death, the last enemy of God, by being full of life to reign in life (Num. 6:6-7, 9; 2 Cor. 5:4; Rom. 5:17; 8:6, 11).

5. Our will must be subdued and resurrected by Christ to be like the tower of David, the armory for spiritual warfare (S. S. 4:4; cf. 1 Chron. 11:22).

C. The inoculator is an athlete (2 Tim. 2:5):

1. We must run the Christian race until we finish our course, fully accomplishing our ministry in the unique ministry of God's economy so that we may receive Christ as our prize (1 Cor. 9:24-25).

2. We must subdue our body and make it a conquered captive to serve us as a slave for the fulfilling of our holy purpose, not by our own effort but by the Spirit (vv. 26-27; Rom. 8:13).

3. We must live the normal church life by pursuing Christ as righteousness, faith, love, and peace with those who call on the Lord out of a pure heart (2 Tim. 2:22).

Day 3   D. The inoculator is a farmer (v. 6):

1. The church is God's farm, God's cultivated land, and we are God's fellow workers, working together with Him by an all-fitting life to sow the seed of life into people and to

water them with the Spirit of life by His
healthy words (1 Cor. 3:6, 9; 2 Cor. 6:1a; Luke
8:11; John 7:38; 6:63; 2 Cor. 3:6):

a. The word of God, as a grain of wheat, dispenses God as life into us to nourish us; it
is also a fire and a hammer to purify us
and break down our self, our natural life,
our flesh, our lusts, and our concepts
(Jer. 23:28-29).

b. God has sent forth His word as rain and
snow to water His people in order to
sanctify them, transform them, and conform them to His image that the Body
may be built up (Isa. 55:8-11; John 17:17;
Eph. 5:26).

2. In our contact with the saints, we should
have just one motive—to minister Christ
to them so that they might grow in the
Lord (1 Tim. 5:1-2).

E. The inoculator is a workman (2 Tim. 2:15):

1. To cut straight the word of the truth means
to unfold the word of God in its various
parts rightly and straightly without distortion (as in carpentry).

2. There is the need of the word of the truth,
rightly unfolded, to enlighten the darkened people, inoculate against the poison,
swallow up the death, and bring the distracted back to the proper track (cf. Acts
26:18; Psa. 119:130).

Day 4 **II. Second Corinthians uses five very significant and expressive metaphors to illustrate
how the ministers of the new covenant and
their ministry were constituted, how they
behaved and lived, and how their ministry
was carried out:**

A. The ministers of the new covenant are captives
in a triumphal procession for the celebration of
Christ's victory (2 Cor. 2:12-14):

1. Paul uses the metaphor of a procession held in honor of the victory of a Roman general to illustrate what he was in the ministry (v. 14).

2. Paul and his co-workers had been conquered by Christ and had become His captives in the train of His triumph, celebrating His victory; therefore, Paul's ministry was a triumphal procession of the victorious General, the Lord Jesus, leading many captives (Eph. 4:8; Col. 1:18b):

   a. In our experience, however, much of the time we must admit that instead of being captives to Christ, Christ is a captive to us (cf. Acts 26:14).

   b. A captive of Christ is daily conquered, defeated, and captured by Christ; for this we should pray, "Lord, make me Your captive. Never let me win. Defeat me all the time."

B. The ministers of the new covenant are incense-bearers to scatter the fragrance of Christ (2 Cor. 2:14b-17):

   1. As captives of Christ in Christ's triumphal procession, we are simultaneously incense-bearers; through us God manifests the savor of the knowledge of Christ in every place (v. 14).

   2. Actually, to scatter the incense of Christ is to live Christ (Phil. 1:19-21a).

   3. Because we have been captured, subdued, possessed, and gained by Christ, He has the liberty to saturate us to make us a fragrance of Christ (2 Cor. 2:15).

   4. The ministers of Christ, the lovers of Christ, are prepared to give forth Christ's fragrance in all circumstances and in any kind of environment (S. S. 4:10-16).

   5. Those who scatter the fragrance of Christ are not like the many, adulterating the word

of God for profit; but they speak as out of sincerity, as out of God, before God, and in Christ for the building up of the Body of Christ (2 Cor. 2:17; cf. 13:3).

6. As incense-bearers scattering the fragrance of Christ, we are the ambassadors of Christ (5:20).

Day 5

C. The ministers of the new covenant are letters written with Christ as the content to convey and express Christ (3:1-3):

1. Christ is written into every part of our inner being with the Spirit of the living God to make us His living letters, that He may be expressed, read, and known by others in us (vv. 2-3; cf. Eph. 3:17a).

2. The Spirit of the living God, who is the living God Himself, is not the instrument, like a pen, but the element, like ink used in writing, with which the apostles minister Christ as the content for the writing of living letters that convey Christ (Phil. 1:19; Exo. 30:23-25).

3. The heavenly, compound ink is the compound Spirit, the essence of this Spirit-ink is Christ with all His riches, and we are the pen; to have this ink in our experience, we must enjoy and be thoroughly saturated with Christ as the life-giving Spirit; then we will spontaneously minister Christ to those whom we contact, making them living letters of Christ (Phil. 1:19; 2 Cor. 3:3, 6).

4. On the one hand, the believers were the letter of Christ; on the other hand, they were the letter of the apostles inscribed in their hearts (vv. 2-3).

Day 6

D. The ministers of the new covenant are mirrors beholding and reflecting the glory of Christ in order to be transformed into His glorious image (vv. 16-18; 4:1):

1. Whenever our heart turns to the Lord, the veil is taken away from our heart, and we can behold the Lord of glory with an unveiled face (3:16, 18).
2. Actually, our turned-away heart is the veil; to turn our heart to the Lord is to take away the veil.
3. An unveiled face is an unveiled heart to behold the glory of the Lord (vv. 16, 18; 1 Sam. 16:7; Eph. 1:18a).
4. The glory of God is in the face of Christ, and His face, His person, is the indwelling treasure in our spirit (2 Cor. 4:6-7; 1 Pet. 3:4):
   a. We are earthen vessels who are worthless and fragile, but within our spirit we contain a priceless treasure, the face, the person, of Christ Himself (2 Cor. 2:10; 4:6-7).
   b. In the whole universe, there is nothing so precious as to behold the face of Jesus (Gen. 32:30; Exo. 25:30; 33:11; Psa. 27:4, 8; Rev. 22:4).

E. The ministers of the new covenant are earthen vessels to contain the Christ of glory as the excellent treasure (2 Cor. 4:7):
   1. These vessels are like today's camera, into which Christ, the figure, enters through the flash of God's shining (vv. 4, 6-7).
   2. Christ as the priceless treasure is contained in us, the worthless and fragile vessels; this makes the worthless vessels ministers of the new covenant with a priceless ministry (v. 7; cf. Gen. 4:26).
   3. This treasure, the indwelling Christ, in us, the earthen vessels, is the divine supply and power for the Christian life; God's power is manifested in man's weakness, and man's weakness cannot limit God's power (2 Cor. 4:7; 12:10).
   4. The new covenant ministers are Christ's chosen vessels to contain and express Him (Acts 9:15; Rom. 9:21, 23; cf. 2 Cor. 4:5; Dan. 5:2-3, 23).

Morning Nourishment

2 Tim. **And the things which you have heard from me**
2:2 **through many witnesses, these commit to faithful**
men, who will be competent to teach others also.
1 Tim. **If you lay these things before the brothers, you will**
4:6 **be a good minister of Christ Jesus, being nourished**
with the words of the faith and of the good teaching
which you have closely followed.

The subject of 2 Timothy is inoculation against the decline of
the church....Five specific titles [are] given to the inoculator in
2:1-15....If we read these verses carefully, we shall see that Paul
regarded Timothy and his other co-workers as those who should
be teachers, soldiers, contenders, husbandmen, and workmen.

The more we are empowered in this grace [2 Tim. 2:1], the
more able we shall be to teach others....The things to which Paul
refers [in verse 2] are the healthy words in 1:13. The healthy
words, after being committed to faithful men, become the good
deposit in them (1:14). This word indicates that if someone in a
local church has a deposit of the Lord's healthy words, he should
train the faithful ones, the trustworthy ones, that they also may
have a good deposit from the Lord, thus making them competent
to teach others. (*Life-study of 2 Timothy*, pp. 21-22)

Today's Reading

Paul realized that Timothy had received a good deposit, that
he had been taught and nourished with the riches of grace.
Therefore, he charged Timothy to commit these things to others
who would be faithful and competent to carry on the same ministry. This indicates that more than one person is needed to
carry on the riches of God's New Testament economy. My hope is
that through all these Life-study messages thousands of saints
in the Lord's recovery will receive a good deposit of the riches of
grace concerning God's New Testament economy. Then those
who have received these riches will be able to commit these
things to others. Imagine what the situation would be if the Lord

had ten thousand saints filled with His good deposit, spreading the riches of His economy throughout the earth. No doubt, this would hasten the time of His glorious appearing....In 2 Timothy 2:1 and 2...Paul is burdened to charge Timothy, one who had received such a good deposit, to pass on the riches of grace to others. (*Life-study of 2 Timothy*, pp. 22-23)

When we go out to contact people, we must be persons living a human life in resurrection....The Lord revealed that resurrection is not a matter of time but a matter of His person, because He is the resurrection [John 11:25]....Jesus [in the Gospels] was not a man living a natural life [but a life in resurrection]. He always put His humanity aside. He was in His humanity, yet He did not live a life of His humanity. Every day while He was on the earth, Jesus was in the flesh, but that flesh was in resurrection. Apparently, He was a Nazarene, a natural Galilean. He was in that flesh. But His living was in a humanity in resurrection.

A charming person must be very warm, not cold. Those who are charming in their natural humanity, however, are not real. Actually, they are performers, like actors in a theater. When you get close to a charming man, you will find out that he actually is not that charming. He was born with a mask. When the mask is taken away, he is different. To cherish people in our natural humanity is not genuine. This is why we must cherish people in the humanity of Jesus. The Lord's charming and cherishing are not natural but are by His resurrection life in humanity.

As members of the vital groups, we must be such persons. Then we will cherish people. When we contact people, they will be touched by us because we are living in resurrection. Then our humanity is not the original humanity but the crucified and resurrected humanity. (*The Vital Groups*, pp. 92-93, 95-96)

Further Reading: Life-study of 2 Timothy, msg. 3; The Vital Groups, msgs. 1, 6-7, 10-11; The Governing and Controlling Vision in the Bible, ch. 3; Experiencing the Mingling of God with Man for the Oneness of the Body of Christ, ch. 5

Enlightenment and inspiration: _____

_____

_____

_____

Morning Nourishment

2 Tim. **Suffer evil with *me* as a good soldier of Christ Jesus.**
2:3-5 **No one serving as a soldier entangles himself with the affairs of this life, that he may please the one who enlisted *him*. And also if anyone contends *in the games*, he is not crowned unless he contends lawfully.**
1 Cor. **For also if the trumpet gives an uncertain sound,**
14:8 **who will prepare himself for battle?**

The apostles considered their ministry a warfare for Christ, just as the priestly service was considered a military service, a warfare, in Numbers 4:23, 30, 35 (lit.). Whenever we minister Christ to others, we find ourselves in a battle. Hence, we should not only be teachers committing the deposit to others, but we should also be soldiers fighting for God's interests.

[In 2 Timothy 2:4] the word for life in Greek is *bios*, indicating the physical life in this age. To fight a good fight (4:7) for the Lord's interests on this earth we must be cleared of any earthly entanglement. The matters of our material, physical life should not entangle us as we are endeavoring to minister Christ to others. This ministry is a fighting, and the fighting requires that we be free from entanglement. On the one hand, the priestly service is a ministry to God; on the other hand, it is a warfare against God's enemies. As the priests were bearing the ark of testimony, they had to be prepared to fight against those who might attack this testimony. (*Life-study of 2 Timothy,* pp. 23-24)

Today's Reading

The apostle Paul inserted this verse [1 Cor. 14:8] with the word "battle" in it. No one among us would consider a battle a small thing. An army that is fighting a battle needs the morale, a fighting unity. In order to maintain this morale even a little dissension concerning the smallest matter has to be killed. If that little dissenting talk is not killed, the morale will be annulled. There will be no more morale, and surely the army will lose the fight, the battle. This warns me concerning the seriousness of the Lord's ministry.

The Lord's ministry is like the sounding of the trumpet for the army to go on to war (Num. 10:9; Judg. 7:18),...a matter of a battle.

We are doing something more serious than any battle on this earth. We are fighting against God's enemy, Satan. The church is God's army, and this is fully revealed and illustrated in many aspects in Ephesians 6. Ephesians...tells us that the Body of Christ, the church, is the fullness of the One who fills all in all (1:22-23),...the new man created in Christ on the cross (2:15-16), ...the kingdom of God, the household of the very God (2:19), and the wife of Christ, His counterpart (5:24-25)....The church, the Body of Christ, with such a tremendous status, is [also] a warrior to fight against God's enemy. Whatever Christ is and whatever Christ has done should be used and applied as aspects of the armor of God. We have to wear Christ as our breast-plate (6:14) and as our shield (v. 16). We have to have our loins girded with Christ (v. 14), and we have to wear Christ as a pair of shoes for our standing to fight the battle (v. 15). The church is not a mere group of people collected together. The church is a universal and divine army fighting for God in the universe against His enemy. (*Elders' Training, Book 7: One Accord for the Lord's Move,* pp. 76-77)

In 2 Timothy 2:5 Paul likens Timothy to an athlete contending in the games....At the same time Timothy was to be a teacher and a soldier, he was also to be an athlete. A soldier must fight to win the victory, whereas an athlete must contend lawfully to receive the crown. It is important for a runner in a race to run fast. That is not the time for him to exercise patience....When it comes to running the race to win the crown, we should not wait. On the contrary, we should run to reach the goal. (*Life-study of 2 Timothy,* p. 24)

Further Reading: The Recovery of God's House and God's City, chs. 6, 8; *Life-study of Numbers,* msgs. 9-10; *Life and Building as Portrayed in the Song of Songs,* ch. 6; *Elders' Training, Book 7: One Accord for the Lord's Move,* ch. 6

Enlightenment and inspiration: _____

_____

_____

_____

Morning Nourishment

2 Tim. **The laboring farmer must be the first to partake of**
2:6 **the fruit.**
15 **Be diligent to present yourself approved to God, an**
     unashamed workman, cutting straight the word of
     the truth.

[In 2 Timothy 2:6]…Paul likens Timothy to a husbandman,
a farmer. Just as a soldier must win the victory and an athlete
must receive the crown, so a husbandman must partake of the
fruits, the food. This requires patience. As athletes we should
be quick, but as farmers we need to be patient. If out of impa-
tience a farmer would pluck up the tiny sprouts, his crop would
be ruined. Likewise, if he drives his cattle too much, he may
hurt them. With both crops and livestock, farmers must learn
to have patience. (*Life-study of 2 Timothy*, p. 24)

Today's Reading

In [2 Timothy 2:15] Paul indicates that the inoculator is to be
a workman. As a carpenter, this workman must cut straight the
word of the truth. This means to unfold the word of God in its
various parts rightly and straightly without distortion. Just as a
carpenter has the skill to cut wood in a straight way, so the
Lord's workman needs the skill to cut straight the word of truth.
This is necessary because in the decline of the church so many
truths are twisted and presented in a warped, biased form.

"Contentions of words" (2:14), "profane, vain babblings" (v. 16),
the eating word of gangrene (v. 17), and "foolish questionings"
(v. 23) are often very much used by the devil (v. 26) in the down
current among the churches to produce contentions (v. 23), to
ruin the hearers (v. 14), to promote ungodliness (v. 16), and to
overthrow people's faith (v. 18). Hence, there is the need of the
word of the truth rightly unfolded to enlighten the darkened
ones, inoculate against the poison, swallow up the death, and
bring the distracted back to the right track.

Among Christians today, only the superficial aspects of the

truth are not twisted. Virtually all the deeper things of the truth have been distorted....Therefore, we should be not only teachers, soldiers, contenders, and farmers, but also workmen, carpenters, cutting straight the word of the truth. The truth here does not merely denote biblical doctrine; it refers to the contents and the reality of God's New Testament economy. The main elements of this truth are Christ as the mystery of God and the embodiment of God and the church as the mystery of Christ and the Body of Christ. We all need to learn to cut straight the word of truth with respect to Christ and the church.

Certain of the Brethren teachers interpret Paul's word about cutting straight the word of truth to mean dividing the Bible into various dispensations: innocence, conscience, human government, promise, law, grace, and kingdom. The Bible can be understood according to these dispensations. However, arranging the Word into dispensations is not what Paul means in 2:15....We need to understand the word truth in this verse according to its usage in the three books of 1 and 2 Timothy and Titus. First Timothy 3:15 says that the church is "the pillar and base of the truth." This truth is the mystery of godliness, God manifest in the flesh. The church should bear, uphold, this truth, this reality....First Timothy 2:4 says that God "desires all men to be saved and to come to the full knowledge of the truth." The word of the truth in 2 Timothy 2:15 refers to the healthy words of God's New Testament economy. As workmen, we should learn not merely to divide the Bible into dispensations. This is too superficial....If we consider these books carefully, we shall see that truth here denotes the reality of the contents of the New Testament economy of God. Therefore, to cut straight the word of the truth is to unfold without bias or distortion the reality of God's economy revealed in the New Testament. (*Life-study of 2 Timothy,* pp. 26-28)

Further Reading: Life-study of 1 Timothy, msg. 9; *Life-study of 2 Timothy,* msgs. 4-5

Enlightenment and inspiration: _____

_____

_____

_____

Morning Nourishment

2 Cor. **But thanks be to God, who always leads us in tri-**
2:14-16 **umph in the Christ and manifests the savor of the**
knowledge of Him through us in every place. For
we are a fragrance of Christ to God in those who
are being saved and in those who are perishing: To
some a savor out of death unto death, and to the
others a savor out of life unto life....

In the apostles' speaking concerning their ministry for
God's new covenant, five very significant and expressive metaphors are used to illustrate how they, as the ministers of the
new covenant, and their ministry are constituted, how they
behave and live, and how their ministry is carried out. These
metaphors are: captives in a triumphant procession for the celebration of Christ's victory (2 Cor. 2:14a); incense-bearers to
scatter the fragrance of Christ (2:14b-16); letters written with
Christ as the content (3:1-3); mirrors beholding and reflecting
the glory of Christ in order to be transformed into His glorious
image (3:18); earthen vessels to contain the Christ of glory as
the excellent treasure (4:7). (*Life-study of 2 Corinthians,* p. 82)

Today's Reading

Concerning 2 Corinthians 2:14, Conybeare has this to say:
"The verb here used means to lead a man as a captive in a triumphal procession; the full phrase means, to lead captive in a
triumph over the enemies of Christ....God is celebrating His
triumph over His enemies; Paul (who had been so great an
opponent of the gospel) is a captive following in the train of the
triumphal procession, yet (at the same time, by a characteristic
change of metaphor) an incense-bearer, scattering incense
(which was always done on these occasions) as the procession
moves on. Some of the conquered enemies were put to death
when the procession reached the Capitol; to them the smell of
the incense was an odor of death unto death; to the rest who
were spared, an odor of life unto life." The same metaphor is

used in Colossians 2:15. God always leads the apostles in such
a triumphant way in their ministry. The word "us" [in 2 Corinthians 2:14] refers to the conquered captives in the train of
Christ's triumph, celebrating and participating in Christ's triumph. The apostles are such captives; their move as captives of
Christ in their ministry for Him is God's celebration of Christ's
victory over His enemies.

In verse 14 Paul also likens himself and his co-workers to
incense-bearers scattering the savor of the knowledge of Christ
in His triumphant ministry as in a triumphal procession.…
Concerning the phrase "the savor of the knowledge," Vincent
says, "According to the Greek usage, savor and knowledge are in
apposition, so that the knowledge of Christ is symbolized as an
odor communicating its nature and efficacy through the apostle's work." The apostles' excellent knowledge of Christ became a
sweet savor. (*Life-study of 2 Corinthians,* pp. 40, 42)

In your experience who is the captive—Christ or you? Who is
celebrating the victory? Who is defeated—you or Christ? Many
of us have to admit that nearly all the time, Christ our Savior
has been defeated and captured by us, becoming our captive in
the train of the celebration of our fleshly victory.…In so many
things and nearly in all things we are not subdued or conquered
by Christ. It may be that our will, the human will, the self-will,
has never been conquered.…We should consider whether or not
our desire has been conquered by Christ.…You may be seeking
the Lord, yet be seeking Him according to your will. On the one
hand, you are a seeker of the Lord, but on the other hand, you
are an opponent to Christ. We all must realize that we first have
to be conquered. We have to be defeated, praying from the
depths of our being, "Lord, defeat me. Be merciful to me and
never let me have the victory.…Lord, keep me defeated." (*An
Autobiography of a Person in the Spirit,* pp. 26-27)

Further Reading: Life-study of 2 Corinthians, msgs. 5, 18; *An
Autobiography of a Person in the Spirit,* chs. 2-3*

Enlightenment and inspiration: _____

_____

_____

_____

Morning Nourishment

2 Cor. You are our letter, inscribed in our hearts, known and
3:2-3 read by all men, since you are being manifested that
you are a letter of Christ ministered by us, inscribed
not with ink but with the Spirit of the living God; not
in tablets of stone but in tablets of hearts of flesh.
6 Who has also made us sufficient as ministers of a
new covenant, *ministers* not of the letter but of the
Spirit; for the letter kills, but the Spirit gives life.

The believers were the fruit of the apostles' labor, commend-
ing the apostles and their ministry to others. Thus, they became
the apostles' living letters of commendation, written by the
apostles with the indwelling Christ as the content in every part
of their inner being.

The Corinthian believers, as the apostles' living letter of
commendation were inscribed in the apostles' hearts. Thus,
they were carried by the apostles and could not possibly be sev-
ered from them. They were in the apostles' hearts (2 Cor. 7:3),
brought by them everywhere as their living commendation.
(*Life-study of 2 Corinthians*, p. 47)

Today's Reading

A letter of Christ is one composed of Christ as the content to
convey and express Christ. All believers in Christ should be such a
living letter of Christ that others may read and know Christ in
their being. These letters are written by the ministry of the apostles. The apostles are filled with Christ so that their ministry spontaneously ministers Christ to those they contact, inscribing Christ
in their heart and making them living letters conveying Christ.

Our heart, as the composition of our conscience (the leading
part of our spirit), mind, emotion, and will, is the tablet upon
which the living letters of Christ are written with the living Spirit
of God. This implies that Christ is written into every part of our
inner being with the Spirit of the living God to make us His living
letters, that He may be expressed in us and read by others in us.

As Paul was ministering to the believers at Corinth, the writing was taking place both in the hearts of the believers and also in his own heart....Therefore, the same letter was written in Paul's heart that was written in the hearts of the believers. Wherever Paul went, this letter was in him, for the believers had become his letter. On the one hand, they were the letter of Christ; on the other hand, they were the letter of the apostles inscribed in their hearts. (*Life-study of 2 Corinthians,* pp. 47, 49-51)

The Corinthians...were the letters of Christ who had been inscribed by the apostles with the Spirit of the living God as the divine, heavenly ink (3:3). The Spirit is neither the writer nor the pen but the writing ink to write Christ into our being. The more we are written on with the Spirit, the more of the heavenly ink we have....The Spirit as the ink brings the heavenly element into us to make this element one with us.

The Spirit is the ink, and the content of the ink is Christ with His person, work, and attainments. This heavenly ink is a compound of all the elements of Christ. The more we are inscribed with this ink, the more we have the elements of Christ dispensed into us. Then we become a letter of Christ with Christ as our content.

The Spirit as the compound ink adds the substance of Christ into us and saturates us with the essence of Christ. Then we have the substance of Christ to really express Christ. There may not be much of Christ in our mind, emotion, and will. But when we are written on with the Spirit again and again, the essence of Christ is dispensed into us. Then our mind, emotion, and will express Christ because Christ has been inscribed into these parts of our soul. The essence and elements of Christ are added into us by the writing of the heavenly ink, the compound Spirit. (*The Experience of Christ as Life for the Building Up of the Church,* p. 102)

Further Reading: Life-study of 2 Corinthians, msgs. 6, 19; *The Experience of Christ as Life for the Building Up of the Church,* chs. 12-13

Enlightenment and inspiration: _____

_____

_____

_____

Morning Nourishment

2 Cor. **But whenever *their heart* turns to the Lord, the**
3:16 **veil is taken away.**
4:6-7 **Because the God who said, Out of darkness light**
shall shine, is the One who shined in our hearts to
illuminate the knowledge of the glory of God in the
face of Jesus Christ. But we have this treasure in
earthen vessels that the excellency of the power
may be of God and not out of us.

When their heart is away from the Lord, the veil lies on their heart [2 Cor. 3:15]. When their heart turns to the Lord, the veil is taken away. Actually, their turned-away heart is the veil. To turn their heart to the Lord is to take away the veil. (3:16, footnote 1)

Christ as the image of God is the effulgence of His glory (Heb. 1:3). Hence, the gospel of Christ is the gospel of His glory that illuminates and shines forth. Satan, the god of this age, has blinded the minds and the thoughts of the unbelievers, so that the illumination of the gospel of Christ's glory should not shine into their hearts. This is similar to covering the lens of a camera so that the light cannot shine into the camera.

What Paul describes in 2 Corinthians 4:4 is a kind of spiritual photography. We are like cameras with a lens and a shutter. When the shutter is pressed, there is a way for the light with the object, the figure, the image, to shine into the camera and be impressed on the film. The light brings the figure to the film and forms an image on it. However, if the lens of the camera is covered, there is no way for the light to shine into the camera. (*Life-study of 2 Corinthians*, p. 78)

Today's Reading

The unveiled face in 2 Corinthians 3:18 is the uncovered mind in chapter four. According to Paul's concept, these two things are one. To have an unveiled face, therefore, is to have an uncovered mind. It is to be like a camera open to the shining of light.

As light shines into us, it brings in the image of Christ. This illumination shines into our spirit through our mind. Our spirit can be compared to the film. When the shining comes into us through our open mind, it reaches our spirit and brings the figure of Christ, the image of God, into us. In the church we are practicing such a spiritual and heavenly photography.... The purpose of God's shining in our hearts...is to illumine us so that we may know the glory in Christ's face.

Suppose you are preaching the gospel to an unbeliever. He nods and says that he believes in the Lord Jesus and receives Him as Savior. Do not assume that he has truly been saved. You need to ask if he has called on the Lord, thereby having direct contact with Him. If such an unbeliever would call on the name of the Lord Jesus, he would be brought to the face of Christ and immediately have personal contact with Him.

God's shining in our hearts brings into us a treasure, the Christ of glory, who is the embodiment of God to be our life and our everything [4:7]. But we who contain this treasure are earthen vessels, worthless and fragile. A priceless treasure is contained in the worthless vessels. This has made the worthless vessels ministers of the new covenant with a priceless ministry. It is by the divine power in resurrection. The excellence of the power is surely of God and not of us.

This treasure, the indwelling Christ, in us, the earthen vessels, is the divine source of the supply for the Christian life. It is by the excellent power of this treasure that the apostles as the ministers of the new covenant are capable of living a crucified life that the resurrection life of Christ whom they minister may be manifested. Thus, they manifest the truth for the shining of the gospel. (*Life-study of 2 Corinthians,* pp. 78, 80-83)

Further Reading: Life-study of 2 Corinthians, msgs. 4, 7-10, 23-24;
  An Autobiography of a Person in the Spirit, chs. 4-6; *The Stream
  Magazine, Book Two,* pp. 1324-1325; *The Conclusion of the New
  Testament,* msg. 112; *The Organic Aspect of God's Salvation,* ch. 4

Enlightenment and inspiration: _____

_____

_____

_____

Hymns, #403

1   Live Thyself, Lord Jesus, through me,
     For my very life art Thou;
   Thee I take to all my problems
     As the full solution now.
   Live Thyself, Lord Jesus, through me,
     In all things Thy will be done;
   I but a transparent vessel
     To make visible the Son.

2   Consecrated is Thy temple,
     Purged from every stain and sin;
   May Thy flame of glory now be
     Manifested from within.
   Let the earth in solemn wonder
     See my body willingly
   Offered as Thy slave obedient,
     Energized alone by Thee.

3   Every moment, every member,
     Girded, waiting Thy command;
   Underneath the yoke to labor
     Or be laid aside as planned.
   When restricted in pursuing,
     No disquiet will beset;
   Underneath Thy faithful dealing
     Not a murmur or regret.

4   Ever tender, quiet, restful,
     Inclinations put away,
   That Thou may for me choose freely
     As Thy finger points the way.
   Live Thyself, Lord Jesus, through me,
     For my very life art Thou;
   Thee I take to all my problems
     As the full solution now.

Composition for prophecy with main point and sub-points: _____

_____

_____

_____

_____

_____

_____

_____

_____

_____

_____

_____

_____

_____

_____

_____

_____

_____

_____

_____

_____

_____

_____

_____

_____

_____

_____

_____

_____

_____

_____

_____

_____

_____

_____

_____

_____

A Genuine Church
in the Focus of the Lord's Recovery

Scripture Reading: 1 Cor. 1:2-9; 12:12, 24; 10:17

Day 1

I. **First Corinthians unveils to us a genuine church in the focus of the Lord's recovery, which is the focus of God's economy; Paul, in the opening of his Epistle to the Corinthians, presents a beautiful, marvelous, and excellent portrait of the church of God (1:2-9):**

A. "The church of God"—this is a church that is not only being possessed by God but also has God as its nature and essence, which are divine, general, universal, and eternal (v. 2a).

B. "The church...in Corinth"—this is a church in a city that remains in a definite locality and takes it as its standing, ground, and jurisdiction for its administration in business affairs, and that is physical, particular, local, and temporal in time (v. 2b).

C. "The church...sanctified in Christ Jesus"—this is a church that has been sanctified, made holy, in Christ, having Christ, who is the embodiment of the processed Triune God in His fullness, as its element and sphere (v. 2c).

Day 2

D. The church being composed of the "called saints"— this is the assembly of the saints, the sanctified ones, who have been called out of the satanic world (v. 2d).

E. "With all those who call upon the name of our Lord Jesus Christ in every place"—this long phrase indicates that the church that is genuine is related with all the saints who call upon the name of the Lord Jesus Christ in every place around the globe (v. 2e).

F. The Lord Jesus Christ being "theirs and ours"— this indicates that the church that is genuine has the Lord Jesus Christ as "their" portion, "their" possession of the divine inheritance, for "their" enjoyment (v. 2f).

G. "Grace to you and peace from God our Father and the Lord Jesus Christ"—this indicates that the church that is genuine is under the dispensing of "grace" (the embodiment of the processed Triune God for the enjoyment of Him as grace by His called ones), from God the Father as the source of the Divine Trinity, from the Lord Jesus Christ as the course of the flow of the Divine Trinity, and from the Holy Spirit as the reaching of the flow of the Divine Trinity (not mentioned in word but implied in denotation—2 Cor. 13:14) (1 Cor. 1:3).

H. "Based upon the grace of God which was given to you in Christ Jesus"—this indicates that the church that is genuine has the grace of God given to it in Christ, not the condition in itself, as its base (v. 4).

Day 3

I. "In everything you were enriched in Him...so that you do not lack in any gift"—this indicates that the church that is genuine is enriched in everything in Christ, so that it is not lacking in any gift, the inward initial gift issuing from grace, such as the eternal life and the Holy Spirit (Rom. 6:23; Acts 2:38; Heb. 6:4), not the outward miraculous gifts (1 Cor. 1:5-7a).

J. "Eagerly awaiting the revelation of our Lord Jesus Christ"—this indicates that the church that is genuine should have a normal sign, that is, eagerly awaiting the revelation (the appearing) of our Lord Jesus Christ (v. 7b).

K. "Who [referring to God in verse 4] will also confirm you until the end unreprovable in the day of our Lord Jesus Christ"—this indicates that the church that is genuine needs to grow in life (as mentioned in 3:6) after its initial receiving of grace, so that it will be unreprovable in the day of Christ's coming (1:8).

L. "God is faithful, through whom you were called into the fellowship of His Son, Jesus Christ our Lord"— this indicates that the church that is genuine has been called by God the Father, who is faithful, into the fellowship of, the participation in, His Son Jesus Christ, who is the consummated, all-inclusive, indwelling, life-giving, and dispensing Spirit (15:45b; 2 Cor. 3:17-18), as its divine portion for its enjoyment of the consummated Triune God (1 Cor. 1:9).

Day 4 II. **First Corinthians unveils to us a genuine church in the focus of the Lord's recovery—a meal-offering church life:**

A. The meal offering first typifies Christ in His God-man living and our Christian life as a duplication of His God-man living (Lev. 2:1-16; Psa. 92:10; 1 Pet. 2:21; Rom. 8:2-3, 11, 13):

1. Fine flour, the main element of the meal offering, signifies Christ's humanity, which is fine, perfect, tender, balanced, and right in every way, with no excess and no deficiency; this signifies the beauty and excellence of Christ's human living and daily walk (Lev. 2:1; John 18:38; 19:4, 6b; Luke 2:40; 23:14; Isa. 53:3).

Day 5 2. The oil of the meal offering signifies the Spirit of God as the divine element of Christ (Lev. 2:1; Luke 1:35; 3:22; 4:18; Heb. 1:9).

3. The mingling of fine flour with the oil in the meal offering signifies that Christ's humanity is mingled with the Holy Spirit and that His human nature is mingled with God's divine nature, making Him a God-man, possessing the divine nature and the human nature distinctly, without a third nature being produced (Lev. 2:4-5; Matt. 1:18, 20).

4. The frankincense in the meal offering signifies the fragrance of Christ in His resurrection; that the frankincense was put on the fine flour signifies that Christ's humanity bears the aroma of His resurrection (Lev. 2:1-2; cf. Matt. 2:11; 11:20-30; Luke 10:21):

      a. As portrayed in the four Gospels, Christ lived a life in His humanity mingled with His divinity and expressing resurrection out from His sufferings (cf. John 18:4-8; 19:26-27a).

      b. Christ's Spirit-filled and resurrection-saturated living was a satisfying fragrance to God, giving God rest, peace, joy, enjoyment, and full satisfaction (Lev. 2:2; Luke 4:1; John 11:25; Matt. 3:17; 17:5).

5. Salt, with which the meal offering was seasoned, signifies the death, or the cross, of Christ; salt functions to season, kill germs, and preserve (Lev. 2:13):

      a. The Lord Jesus always lived a life of being salted, a life under the cross (Mark 10:38; John 12:24; Luke 12:49-50).

      b. Even before He was actually crucified, Christ daily lived a crucified life, denying Himself and His natural life and living the Father's life in resurrection (John 6:38; 7:6, 16-18; cf. Gal. 2:20).

      c. The basic factor of God's covenant is the cross, the crucifixion of Christ, signified by salt; it is by the cross that God's covenant is preserved to be an everlasting covenant (cf. Heb. 13:20).

Day 6

6. That the meal offering was without leaven signifies that in Christ there is no sin or any negative thing (Lev. 2:4-5, 11a; 2 Cor. 5:21; Heb. 4:15; 1 Pet. 2:22; Luke 23:14; cf. 1 Cor. 5:6-8).

7. That the meal offering was without honey signifies that in Christ there is no natural affection or natural goodness (Lev. 2:11b; Matt. 10:34-39; 12:46-50; Mark 10:18).

8. If we eat Christ as the meal offering, we will become what we eat and live by what we eat (John 6:57, 63; 1 Cor. 10:17; Phil. 1:19-21a).

9. By exercising our spirit to touch the Spirit consolidated in the Word, we eat the human life and living of Jesus, we are constituted with Jesus, and the human living of Jesus becomes our human living (Eph. 6:17-18; Jer. 15:16; Gal. 6:17).

B. Christ's life and our individual Christian life issue in a totality—the church life as a corporate meal offering; the meal-offering church life is seen in 1 Corinthians (Lev. 2:1-2, 4; 1 Cor. 12:12, 24; 10:17):

1. Christ is the man given to us by God (1:2, 9, 30).

2. Paul's charge to the Corinthians—"be a man" (16:13, lit.)—means that we should have the high, uplifted humanity of Jesus (9:26-27; 13:4-7).

3. The church life is a life of humanity oiled by and with the Spirit and joined to the Spirit (2:4, 12; 3:16; 6:17).

4. The grace of God, which we are enjoying today, is the resurrected Christ as the life-giving Spirit (15:10, 45b):

   a. We must die with Christ to self daily so that we may live with Christ to God daily (vv. 31, 36; John 12:24-26).

   b. We must demonstrate the reality of resurrection by being one with God and having God with us in the state in which we were called (1 Cor. 7:24, 21-22a, 10-13).

   c. We must labor not by our natural life and natural ability but by the Lord as our resurrection life and power (15:10, 58).

5. We must enjoy the crucified Christ as the solution to all the problems in the church (1:9, 18, 22-23a; cf. Mark 15:31-32a).

6. We must enjoy Christ as our unleavened banquet (1 Cor. 5:6b-8).

7. In the church life, the natural life must be killed by the salt, by the cross of Christ (15:10; 12:31; 13:8a; 2 Cor. 5:16).

8. God desires that every local church be a meal
   offering to satisfy Him and fully supply the
   saints day by day; this means that we will eat
   our church life, for the church life will be our
   daily supply.

Matt 13:
   33'
   leaven signifies sin or
   evil things & evil   any negative things
   doctrines.

Morning Nourishment

1 Cor. To the church of God which is in Corinth, to those who
1:2 have been sanctified in Christ Jesus, the called saints,
with all those who call upon the name of our Lord
Jesus Christ in every place, *who is* theirs and ours.

First Corinthians 1:2-9 [is] very striking....No other portion
of the Word contains such a portrait of what a local church is.
This portion is very short; yet, in these eight verses every fea-
ture of a local church can be seen, including its nature, standing, element, sphere, and relationship. There are twelve significant
items presented in these eight verses, each of which deserves
our full attention. These items are very mysterious and full of
spiritual implications and spiritual, hidden, mysterious, and
divine secrets. (*A Genuine Church,* p. 5)

Today's Reading

[First Corinthians 1:2-9] is a condensation of the entire
book, giving us a skeleton of its structure. Although in these
verses Paul speaks concerning the church in Corinth, he does
not speak about its condition...[but its] nature and standing.

When Paul dealt with the church at Corinth, the condition of
the church was negative and miserable, full of divisions, confusion,
errors, and even heresies and rebellion....However, Paul was wise
and logical. Paul loved the church, and he would never depreciate
or defame the church. Often biographers place a handsome portrait of the subject of their book on the opening page in order to give
the reader a positive impression of that person. In the same way,
Paul, in the opening of his epistle to the Corinthians, presented a
beautiful, marvelous, and excellent portrait of the church of God.

Verse 2a says, "To the church of God." This expression indicates that the church not only is being possessed by God, but that
it has God as its nature and essence, which are divine, general,
universal, and eternal. Paul does not refer to the church in Corinth as a pitiful church with troublesome Jewish teachers and
proud philosophical Greeks. Although others may have looked at

the church according to its condition, Paul knew the real nature of the church, so he had the boldness to call it "the church of God."

As the church of God, the church is not only being possessed by God, but has God as its nature and essence, which are divine, general, universal, and eternal. Every element has its nature, and in the nature of the element is its essence. God is the nature and essence of the church. Therefore, the church is divine.

"The church...in Corinth" (v. 2b) was a church in a city, remaining in a definite locality and taking it as its standing, ground, and jurisdiction for its administration in business affairs. As such, it was physical, particular, local, and temporal in time. The church of God to whom Paul wrote was not in the heavens but in Corinth. Corinth was a very sinful, modern Greek city, which was famous for its fornication. However, the church remained in that locality for a local testimony of Christ. A local testimony of Christ is a part of the universal testimony of Christ. The universal testimony is composed of and constituted with the local testimonies.

The church takes a locality as its standing, ground, and jurisdiction for its administration. A local church has an administration which has a jurisdiction for business affairs. The standing, ground, and jurisdiction of the church is physical rather than divine, particular rather than general, local rather than universal, and temporal in time rather than eternal. These are the local aspects of the church.

The church is "sanctified in Christ" (v. 2c), having been sanctified, made holy, in Christ, who is the embodiment of the processed Triune God in His fullness, as its element and sphere. Christ is the embodiment of the processed Triune God in all His fullness. Now we are in this Christ, and we have this Christ as our element and sphere. Just as wood is the element of a table, Christ is the element of the church. He is also the sphere, the realm, of the church. (*A Genuine Church*, pp. 5-9)

Further Reading: A Genuine Church

Enlightenment and inspiration: _____

_____

_____

_____

Morning Nourishment

1 Cor. To the church of God which is in Corinth, to those
1:2-4 who have been sanctified in Christ Jesus, the called
saints, with all those who call upon the name of our
Lord Jesus Christ in every place, *who is* theirs and
ours: Grace to you and peace from God our Father
and the Lord Jesus Christ. I thank my God always
concerning you based upon the grace of God which
was given to you in Christ Jesus.

The church is composed of the "called saints" (1 Cor. 1:2)—the
church of the saints, the sanctified ones, who have been called out
of the satanic world....We are no longer in the world; we are in the
church which is called by God and sanctified in a wonderful person, Christ, who is our element within and our sphere without.

Verse 2 contains five qualifications for a genuine church....[It] is the
church of God, it is the church in a locality, it is sanctified in Christ,...it is
composed of the called saints,...[and it] is related with all the saints
who call upon the name of the Lord...in every place around the globe.
Paul does not address the church as being related to all those who have
been baptized by immersion or all those who speak in tongues or keep
the Sabbath. Rather, the church is related to all those—including the
believers today, those who came before us and those who will come after
us—who call upon the name of our Lord Jesus Christ in every place.

Being related with all the saints keeps us from being sectarian,
isolated, or divided....If we have nothing to do with other believers,
we are not a local church...[but] a local sect, a local division. We
must be open, and our openness must be in every direction. We are
open to all those who call upon the name of the Lord Jesus, regardless of their particular practices. (*A Genuine Church*, pp. 9-11)

Today's Reading

["Theirs and ours"] indicates that the church which is genuine has the Lord Jesus Christ as "their" portion, "their" possession of the divine inheritance, for "their" enjoyment. He is
the portion of all believers in every place (1 Cor. 1:2).

Verse 3...indicates that the church which is genuine is under the dispensing of "grace," which is the embodiment of the processed Triune God for the enjoyment of His called ones, and "peace," the processed Triune God as the issue of the enjoyment of Him as grace by His called ones. Grace and peace are dispensed to the church from God the Father as the source of the Divine Trinity, from the Lord Jesus Christ as the course of the flow of the Divine Trinity, and from the Holy Spirit as the reaching of the flow of the Divine Trinity....Whenever the Father and Son are mentioned, the Spirit is implied. Therefore, the grace and peace is from the Triune God, the Divine Trinity—the divine Father, the divine Son, and the divine Spirit—one God in different aspects, with all the riches of the Divine Trinity.

Verse 4...indicates that the church which is genuine has the grace of God given to it in Christ....The grace of God is not given to the church based upon the spirituality or condition of the church. The grace of God alone is the base for the church....In the New Testament, the phrase "in Christ" is mainly used related to the Triune God (2 Cor. 5:19) and the believers corporately (1 Cor. 1:30). Therefore, the grace of God given to the believers is the Triune God Himself.

The church is standing on the base of grace in order that it may receive further grace. We have received grace as our base, and today we are standing upon grace, not upon our attributes, virtues, or excellencies. Therefore, we are qualified to receive more grace, even grace upon grace. John 1:16 says, "For of His fullness we have all received, and grace upon grace."...We have to thank the Lord that the more storms there are in the church, the more "waves" of grace there are....Moreover, this grace issues in peace. In His Divine Trinity, God is not only grace but peace to us. After receiving grace, we are at peace, and we can say, "Hallelujah, Amen!" We are in the peace because we have enjoyed grace, and we have grace because we have received grace upon grace. (*A Genuine Church*, pp. 11-15)

Further Reading: A Genuine Church

Enlightenment and inspiration: _____

_____

_____

_____

Morning Nourishment

1 Cor. **That in everything you were enriched in Him, in all**
1:5-9 **utterance and all knowledge,...so that you do not**
lack in any gift, eagerly awaiting the revelation of our
Lord Jesus Christ, who will also confirm you until the
end unreprovable in the day of our Lord Jesus Christ.
God is faithful, through whom you were called into
the fellowship of His Son, Jesus Christ our Lord.

The church which is genuine is enriched in everything in
Christ, so that it is not lacking in any gift. The gift referred to
[in verse 7] is the inward initial gift issuing from grace, such as
the eternal life and the Holy Spirit (Rom. 6:23; Acts 2:38; Heb.
6:4), not the outward miraculous gifts. The Triune God as grace
to us issues in and becomes the gift. We have received grace,
and we have the gift which is out of grace, so that we are not
lacking in any gift. (*A Genuine Church*, p. 15)

Today's Reading

[First Corinthians 1:7] indicates that the church which is genuine should have a normal sign, that is, the awaiting of the unveiling, the appearing, of the Lord Jesus Christ. We are not waiting to
get a good car or a high appointment. Rather, since we have received grace upon grace, we are awaiting the unveiling, the appearing, the second coming, of the Lord Jesus Christ from heaven.

[Verse 8] indicates that a genuine church needs to grow in
life, as mentioned in 3:6, after its initial receiving of grace, that it
will be unreprovable in the day of Christ's coming...."Who" in 1:8
refers not to Christ but to God in verse 4. God has given us grace,
and this very God will also confirm us to the end. He is the Alpha
and the Omega. He is the giver of grace at the beginning and the
completer of our growth in life at the end. He will confirm us
until the end, unreprovable in the day of our Lord Jesus Christ.

Verse 9...indicates that the church which is genuine has been
called by God the Father who is faithful into the fellowship of, the
participation in, His Son Jesus Christ, who is the consummated,
all-inclusive, indwelling and life-giving and dispensing Spirit

(1 Cor. 15:45b; 2 Cor. 3:17-18), as its divine portion for its enjoyment of the consummated Triune God....This life-giving Spirit,
the consummated Spirit as the consummation of the Triune God,
is the church's divine portion for its enjoyment of the consummated
Triune God. Moreover, the church is now one spirit with this Spirit.

Through the faithful Triune God, we were called into the fellowship, communion, enjoyment, and participation of Jesus Christ our
Lord. We have been called into an enjoyment, and this enjoyment
is our fellowship. Moreover, this fellowship is Jesus Christ. He is
our portion, both "theirs and ours" (1 Cor. 1:2). We are enjoying the
Son of God as the embodiment of the Triune God in full. Every
meeting of the genuine church is an enjoying and feasting meeting.

[Verse 9 is] a wonderful conclusion to such a portrait of the
church in verses 2 through 8....The One through whom we were
called is the Triune God as indicated by the reference to "God" and
"His Son." Furthermore, Paul's use of the preposition "through" implies a process through which the Triune God passed in order to
call us. The phrase "through whom" is fully defined in Ephesians 1.
Ephesians 1:3-6 is a portion of the Word on the Father's choosing
and predestination, speaking forth God's eternal purpose. Verses 7-
12 go on to speak of the Son's redemption, speaking forth the ac-
complishment of God's eternal purpose. Then verses 13-14 speak
concerning the Spirit's sealing and pledging, speaking forth the application of God's accomplished purpose....Following this, Paul
goes on to pray that the church would know the hope of God's calling (vv. 17-18a). The Father's choosing, the Son's redeeming, and
the Spirit's sealing consummate in our calling....The Father's
choosing was before the foundation of the world, the Son's redeeming was almost two thousand years ago, and the Spirit's sealing be-
gan fifty days after the Lord's resurrection. This was the process
that the Triune God passed through in order to call the genuine
church into the fellowship of the Son, Jesus Christ. (*A Genuine
Church*, pp. 15-20)

Further Reading: A Genuine Church

Enlightenment and inspiration: _____
_____
_____
_____

Morning Nourishment

Rom. For the law of the Spirit of life has freed me in Christ
8:2-3 Jesus from the law of sin and of death....God, send-
ing His own Son in the likeness of the flesh of sin and
concerning sin, condemned sin in the flesh.

11 And if the Spirit of the One who raised Jesus from
the dead dwells in you, He who raised Christ from
the dead will also give life to your mortal bodies
through His Spirit who indwells you.

13 ...If by the Spirit you put to death the practices of
the body, you will live.

When the Lord Jesus was on earth, He was fine flour, He
was oiled with the Holy Spirit, He was always being salted,
and He lived in resurrection, having the flavor of frankincense. But with Him there was neither leaven nor honey.
Therefore, He could be a meal offering.

The situation with us today should be the same. This
means that our Christian life should be a duplication, a xerox
copy, of Christ's life. This is clearly revealed in Romans 8.

Romans 8 puts Christ and us together. Here we have
Christ's humanity (v. 3), the Spirit of life (v. 2), the cross (v. 13),
and resurrection (v. 11) wrapped up together as one. This
shows us the kind of living we should have today. We should
live the same kind of life Christ lived. He was a man, and we
also are human. He was oiled with the Spirit, and we also
have been at least somewhat oiled with the Spirit. We have
been mingled with the Spirit of the One who raised Jesus
from among the dead. Christ was salted, crucified, and we also
should put our natural being to death. Furthermore, Christ
lived in resurrection, and we also may live in resurrection.
(*Life-study of Leviticus,* pp. 138-139)

Today's Reading

Romans 8 definitely reveals that we should be a duplication of Christ as the meal offering. We should be a copy, a
reproduction, of Him and thus be the same as He is. Christ

became a person in the flesh, and we today are persons in the flesh. As a man in the flesh, Christ was oiled with the Spirit. Today we are being oiled by the indwelling Spirit. The Spirit dwells within us to do the work of oiling us. Since the indwelling Spirit is oiling us, we should set our mind on the spirit, not on the flesh (v. 6). Then by the Spirit we should put to death the practices of the body (v. 13). If we do this, we will live, and this life will be a life in resurrection. As a result, we will be suitable to be a meal offering for God's satisfaction.

As the members of Christ, we should be His duplication and live the same kind of life He lived. This is a life of humanity oiled with the Holy Spirit. Day by day we need to be oiled with the Holy Spirit. We should also continually receive the salt; that is, we should receive Christ's cross and put our natural deeds to death. Then we will live in resurrection and have the frankincense for God's satisfaction.

The meal offering is made of fine flour. Fine flour, therefore, is the main element of the meal offering. This fine flour signifies Christ's humanity.

Christ's humanity is fine, but our humanity is rough and coarse. We may appear outwardly to be gentle and nice, but actually we are rough. Among the human race Christ is the only one who is gentle; only He is the fine flour. With Him there is no roughness. His humanity is fine, perfect, balanced, and right in every way. From every angle—front and back, top and bottom, right and left—He is right.

The fine flour is perfect in fineness, evenness, tenderness, and gentleness and is fully balanced, with no excess and no deficiency. This signifies the beauty and excellence of Christ's human living and daily walk. Christ's humanity is perfect. There is no comparison between His humanity and our natural, fallen humanity. (*Life-study of Leviticus,* pp. 139-140, 99-100)

Further Reading: Life-study of Leviticus, msgs. 15, 11

Enlightenment and inspiration: _____

_____

_____

_____

Morning Nourishment

Lev. **And when anyone presents an offering of a meal**
2:1 **offering to Jehovah, his offering shall be of fine flour;**
and he shall pour oil on it and put frankincense on it.
13 And every offering of your meal offering you shall
season with salt, and you shall not omit the salt of
the covenant of your God from your meal offering;
with all your offerings you shall present salt.

The oil of the meal offering signifies the Spirit of God (Luke 4:18; Heb. 1:9). Christ is a man, and as a man He has an excellent humanity. He also has the divine element, which is the Spirit of God. The divine element is in the Spirit of God and is the Spirit of God. As the meal offering, Christ is full of oil. We may even say that He has been "oiled." He has been mingled with oil. This means that His humanity has been mingled with His divinity.... In the meal offering the oil is poured upon the fine flour. This signifies that the Spirit of God was poured upon Christ (Matt. 3:16; John 1:32). (*Life-study of Leviticus,* pp. 100-101)

Today's Reading

Frankincense is sweet smelling and causes people to have a very pleasant feeling. In typology, the frankincense in the meal offering signifies the fragrance of Christ in His resurrection....The frankincense was put upon the fine flour. This signifies that Christ's humanity bears the aroma of His resurrection manifested out from His sufferings (cf. Matt. 11:20-30; Luke 10:21). During the course of His human life, Christ suffered a great deal, but the aroma of His resurrection was manifested out from His sufferings.

In the meal offering there are three elements: the fine flour, the oil, and the frankincense. If we study the four Gospels, we will see that Christ's life consisted mainly of these three elements. The Lord Jesus continually lived and walked in these three things—in His humanity mingled with His divinity and expressing His resurrection.

If we keep this in mind as we read the Gospels, we will see what kind of person Christ was while He lived on earth. He was a person with the highest and best humanity. This humanity was "oiled," for it was mingled with His divinity. In His human living He expressed not His sufferings but resurrection. This resurrection is the frankincense, the fragrant aroma, the sweet savor, in the universe. Nothing is as sweet, as fragrant, as this aroma of resurrection.

A satisfying fragrance is a sweet savor; it is a fragrance that gives rest, peace, joy, enjoyment, and full satisfaction. The rich elements of the meal offering—Christ's humanity, divinity, and His excellent, perfect, Spirit-filled, and resurrection-saturated living—are a fragrance that gives God rest, peace, joy, enjoyment, and full satisfaction.

The fourth element of the meal offering is salt. In typology salt signifies the death, or the cross, of Christ. Salt seasons, kills germs, and preserves. This is the effect of the cross of Christ.

The salt [in verse 13] is not common; it is the salt of the covenant of God, the covenant which is incorruptible and unchangeable. This salt seasons, kills germs, and preserves.

Thus far, in the meal offering we have seen the Spirit (the oil), Christ's resurrection (the frankincense), and Christ's humanity (the fine flour), but we have not yet seen the death of Christ. The death of Christ, the cross, is signified by the salt. The salt in the meal offering therefore refers to the death of Christ, to the cross.

If we have adequate salt in the church, ambition and natural affection will be crossed out. As long as the cross is here, salt is here; and as long as salt is here, the germs will die. As long as the cross is here, ambition and natural affection will be crossed out. I hope that this will be the experience of us all. We should not have ambition, and we should not have natural affection. We should have only the crossing out of the Lord's death. Then we will have pure humility and pure love. We will be pure, and we will live a life like that of the Lord Jesus when He was on earth, a life without leaven and honey but full of salt. (*Life-study of Leviticus,* pp. 100-102, 108, 133, 116-117)

Further Reading: Life-study of Leviticus, msgs. 12-13

Enlightenment and inspiration: _____

_____

_____

_____

Morning Nourishment

Lev. No meal offering that you present to Jehovah shall be
2:11 made with leaven, for you shall not burn any leaven
      or any honey as an offering by fire to Jehovah.
1 Cor. Purge out the old leaven that you may be a new
5:7-8 lump, even as you are unleavened; for our Passover,
      Christ, also has been sacrificed. So then let us keep
      the feast...with the unleavened *bread* of sincerity
      and truth.
10:17 Seeing that there is one bread, we who are many
      are one Body; for we all partake of the one bread.

The meal offering is to have neither leaven nor honey. Leaven signifies sin and other negative things. In the Gospels the Lord Jesus speaks of the leaven of the Pharisees, the leaven of the Sadducees, and the leaven of Herod (Matt. 16:6, 11-12; Luke 12:1; Mark 8:15).

Honey signifies the natural human life. It signifies our natural life, not in its bad aspect but in its good aspect. We should not think that people are always bad, for sometimes they are very good. But this natural goodness is honey. Hatred is leaven, but natural love is honey. Likewise, pride is leaven, but natural humility is honey. (*Life-study of Leviticus*, p. 133)

Today's Reading

The meal offering is to have neither leaven nor honey. ...Honey seems to be different from leaven. However, after a period of time honey can ferment, and this fermentation will issue in leaven. This indicates that whether we are good or bad, the result will eventually be the same. This is the reason Genesis 2 speaks of the tree of the knowledge of good and evil....We may use divorce as an illustration of the fermentation of honey. With a marriage that ends in divorce, a certain kind of honey—natural love—has fermented and issued in leaven. From this illustration we see that the issue of both hatred, which is leaven, and natural love, which is honey, is the same. The negative things are leaven, and the good aspects of the natural life signified by honey eventually ferment and become leaven.

The life Christ lived on earth was a life without leaven and without honey, and we should live the same kind of life today. We need to have the four positive elements—fine flour, oil, frankincense, and salt—but not the two negative elements—leaven and honey. If this is our situation, we will be a proper meal offering, an offering composed of humanity oiled with divinity in resurrection through Christ's death and without leaven and honey. This kind of life is food to satisfy God and also to nourish us as God's serving ones.

The church life is a corporate meal offering signified by the one bread in 1 Corinthians 10:17....This bread, or cake, signifies the corporate life....We enjoy this corporate life when we partake of the Lord's table....[We] partake of the bread and the cup with the saints. This is a matter of fellowship [v. 16]....We partake of the bread and of the cup in a corporate way. This corporate partaking is a sign of the church life; it is also a testimony of the church life....For this corporate life we need to be a man who is oiled with the Holy Spirit, who lives a life under the cross with the resurrection of Christ as the frankincense, and who does not have leaven or honey. This is the church life as a meal offering.

In this meal offering the top portion is for God's enjoyment, and the remainder is for us to take as our daily food in our service to God....God wants to have a meal offering in every locality. He desires that every local church be a meal offering that satisfies Him and that fully supplies the saints day by day. Our hunger is satisfied not only by Christ but also by the church life...[as] a corporate meal offering, with the top portion for God and the remainder for us. Therefore, we are fed by and with the church life. The church life is the meal offering to be our daily supply. Hallelujah for the meal offering church life! (*Life-study of Leviticus*, pp. 133-134, 151-152)

Further Reading: Life-study of Leviticus, msg. 16; The Practical Points concerning Blending, ch. 2

Enlightenment and inspiration: ____ meal offering

____(1) fine flour

____(2) oil

____(3) frankincense

(4) salt

Hymns, #631

1 If I'd know Christ's risen power,
   I must ever love the Cross;
   Life from death alone arises;
   There's no gain except by loss.

   If no death, no life,
   If no death, no life;
   Life from death alone arises;
   If no death, no life.

2 If I'd have Christ formed within me,
   I must breathe my final breath,
   Live within the Cross's shadow,
   Put my soul-life e'er to death.

3 If God thru th' Eternal Spirit
   Nail me ever with the Lord;
   Only then as death is working
   Will His life thru me be poured.

Composition for prophecy with main point and sub-points: _____

Reading Schedule for the Recovery Version of the Old Testament with Footnotes

Wk.	Lord's Day	Monday	Tuesday	Wednesday	Thursday	Friday	Saturday
1	☐ Gen 1:1-5	☐ 1:6-23	☐ 1:24-31	☐ 2:1-9	☐ 2:10-25	☐ 3:1-13	☐ 3:14-24
2	☐ 4:1-26	☐ 5:1-32	☐ 6:1-22	☐ 7:1—8:3	☐ 8:4-22	☐ 9:1-29	☐ 10:1-32
3	☐ 11:1-32	☐ 12:1-20	☐ 13:1-18	☐ 14:1-24	☐ 15:1-21	☐ 16:1-16	☐ 17:1-27
4	☐ 18:1-33	☐ 19:1-38	☐ 20:1-18	☐ 21:1-34	☐ 22:1-24	☐ 23:1—24:27	☐ 24:28-67
5	☐ 25:1-34	☐ 26:1-35	☐ 27:1-46	☐ 28:1-22	☐ 29:1-35	☐ 30:1-43	☐ 31:1-55
6	☐ 32:1-32	☐ 33:1—34:31	☐ 35:1-29	☐ 36:1-43	☐ 37:1-36	☐ 38:1—39:23	☐ 40:1—41:13
7	☐ 41:14-57	☐ 42:1-38	☐ 43:1-34	☐ 44:1-34	☐ 45:1-28	☐ 46:1-34	☐ 47:1-31
8	☐ 48:1-22	☐ 49:1-15	☐ 49:16-33	☐ 50:1-26	☐ Exo 1:1-22	☐ 2:1-25	☐ 3:1-22
9	☐ 4:1-31	☐ 5:1-23	☐ 6:1-30	☐ 7:1-25	☐ 8:1-32	☐ 9:1-35	☐ 10:1-29
10	☐ 11:1-10	☐ 12:1-14	☐ 12:15-36	☐ 12:37-51	☐ 13:1-22	☐ 14:1-31	☐ 15:1-27
11	☐ 16:1-36	☐ 17:1-16	☐ 18:1-27	☐ 19:1-25	☐ 20:1-26	☐ 21:1-36	☐ 22:1-31
12	☐ 23:1-33	☐ 24:1-18	☐ 25:1-22	☐ 25:23-40	☐ 26:1-14	☐ 26:15-37	☐ 27:1-21
13	☐ 28:1-21	☐ 28:22-43	☐ 29:1-21	☐ 29:22-46	☐ 30:1-10	☐ 30:11-38	☐ 31:1-17
14	☐ 31:18—32:35	☐ 33:1-23	☐ 34:1-35	☐ 35:1-35	☐ 36:1-38	☐ 37:1-29	☐ 38:1-31
15	☐ 39:1-43	☐ 40:1-38	☐ Lev 1:1-17	☐ 2:1-16	☐ 3:1-17	☐ 4:1-35	☐ 5:1-19
16	☐ 6:1-30	☐ 7:1-38	☐ 8:1-36	☐ 9:1-24	☐ 10:1-20	☐ 11:1-47	☐ 12:1-8
17	☐ 13:1-28	☐ 13:29-59	☐ 14:1-18	☐ 14:19-32	☐ 14:33-57	☐ 15:1-33	☐ 16:1-17
18	☐ 16:18-34	☐ 17:1-16	☐ 18:1-30	☐ 19:1-37	☐ 20:1-27	☐ 21:1-24	☐ 22:1-33
19	☐ 23:1-22	☐ 23:23-44	☐ 24:1-23	☐ 25:1-23	☐ 25:24-55	☐ 26:1-24	☐ 26:25-46
20	☐ 27:1-34	☐ Num 1:1-54	☐ 2:1-34	☐ 3:1-51	☐ 4:1-49	☐ 5:1-31	☐ 6:1-27
21	☐ 7:1-41	☐ 7:42-88	☐ 7:89—8:26	☐ 9:1-23	☐ 10:1-36	☐ 11:1-35	☐ 12:1—13:33
22	☐ 14:1-45	☐ 15:1-41	☐ 16:1-50	☐ 17:1—18:7	☐ 18:8-32	☐ 19:1-22	☐ 20:1-29
23	☐ 21:1-35	☐ 22:1-41	☐ 23:1-30	☐ 24:1-25	☐ 25:1-18	☐ 26:1-65	☐ 27:1-23
24	☐ 28:1-31	☐ 29:1-40	☐ 30:1—31:24	☐ 31:25-54	☐ 32:1-42	☐ 33:1-56	☐ 34:1-29
25	☐ 35:1-34	☐ 36:1-13	☐ Deut 1:1-46	☐ 2:1-37	☐ 3:1-29	☐ 4:1-49	☐ 5:1-33
26	☐ 6:1—7:26	☐ 8:1-20	☐ 9:1-29	☐ 10:1-22	☐ 11:1-32	☐ 12:1-32	☐ 13:1—14:21

Reading Schedule for the Recovery Version of the Old Testament with Footnotes

Wk.	Lord's Day	Monday	Tuesday	Wednesday	Thursday	Friday	Saturday
27	☐ 14:22—15:23	☐ 16:1-22	☐ 17:1—18:8	☐ 18:9—19:21	☐ 20:1—21:17	☐ 21:18—22:30	☐ 23:1-25
28	☐ 24:1-22	☐ 25:1-19	☐ 26:1-19	☐ 27:1-26	☐ 28:1-68	☐ 29:1-29	☐ 30:1—31:29
29	☐ 31:30—32:52	☐ 33:1-29	☐ 34:1-12	☐ Josh 1:1-18	☐ 2:1-24	☐ 3:1-17	☐ 4:1-24
30	☐ 5:1-15	☐ 6:1-27	☐ 7:1-26	☐ 8:1-35	☐ 9:1-27	☐ 10:1-43	☐ 11:1—12:24
31	☐ 13:1-33	☐ 14:1—15:63	☐ 16:1—18:28	☐ 19:1-51	☐ 20:1—21:45	☐ 22:1-34	☐ 23:1—24:33
32	☐ Judg 1:1-36	☐ 2:1-23	☐ 3:1-31	☐ 4:1-24	☐ 5:1-31	☐ 6:1-40	☐ 7:1-25
33	☐ 8:1-35	☐ 9:1-57	☐ 10:1—11:40	☐ 12:1—13:25	☐ 14:1—15:20	☐ 16:1-31	☐ 17:1—18:31
34	☐ 19:1-30	☐ 20:1-48	☐ 21:1-25	☐ Ruth 1:1-22	☐ 2:1-23	☐ 3:1-18	☐ 4:1-22
35	☐ 1 Sam 1:1-28	☐ 2:1-36	☐ 3:1—4:22	☐ 5:1—6:21	☐ 7:1—8:22	☐ 9:1-27	☐ 10:1—11:15
36	☐ 12:1—13:23	☐ 14:1-52	☐ 15:1-35	☐ 16:1-23	☐ 17:1-58	☐ 18:1-30	☐ 19:1-24
37	☐ 20:1-42	☐ 21:1—22:23	☐ 23:1—24:22	☐ 25:1-44	☐ 26:1-25	☐ 27:1—28:25	☐ 29:1—30:31
38	☐ 31:1-13	☐ 2 Sam 1:1-27	☐ 2:1-32	☐ 3:1-39	☐ 4:1—5:25	☐ 6:1-23	☐ 7:1-29
39	☐ 8:1—9:13	☐ 10:1—11:27	☐ 12:1-31	☐ 13:1-39	☐ 14:1-33	☐ 15:1—16:23	☐ 17:1—18:33
40	☐ 19:1-43	☐ 20:1—21:22	☐ 22:1-51	☐ 23:1-39	☐ 24:1-25	☐ 1 Kings 1:1-19	☐ 1:20-53
41	☐ 2:1-46	☐ 3:1-28	☐ 4:1-34	☐ 5:1—6:38	☐ 7:1-22	☐ 7:23-51	☐ 8:1-36
42	☐ 8:37-66	☐ 9:1-28	☐ 10:1-29	☐ 11:1-43	☐ 12:1-33	☐ 13:1-34	☐ 14:1-31
43	☐ 15:1-34	☐ 16:1—17:24	☐ 18:1-46	☐ 19:1-21	☐ 20:1-43	☐ 21:1—22:53	☐ 2 Kings 1:1-18
44	☐ 2:1—3:27	☐ 4:1-44	☐ 5:1—6:33	☐ 7:1-20	☐ 8:1-29	☐ 9:1-37	☐ 10:1-36
45	☐ 11:1—12:21	☐ 13:1—14:29	☐ 15:1-38	☐ 16:1-20	☐ 17:1-41	☐ 18:1-37	☐ 19:1-37
46	☐ 20:1—21:26	☐ 22:1-20	☐ 23:1-37	☐ 24:1—25:30	☐ 1 Chron 1:1-54	☐ 2:1—3:24	☐ 4:1—5:26
47	☐ 6:1-81	☐ 7:1-40	☐ 8:1-40	☐ 9:1-44	☐ 10:1—11:47	☐ 12:1-40	☐ 13:1—14:17
48	☐ 15:1—16:43	☐ 17:1-27	☐ 18:1—19:19	☐ 20:1—21:30	☐ 22:1—23:32	☐ 24:1—25:31	☐ 26:1-32
49	☐ 27:1-34	☐ 28:1—29:30	☐ 2 Chron 1:1-17	☐ 2:1—3:17	☐ 4:1—5:14	☐ 6:1-42	☐ 7:1—8:18
50	☐ 9:1—10:19	☐ 11:1—12:16	☐ 13:1—15:19	☐ 16:1—17:19	☐ 18:1—19:11	☐ 20:1-37	☐ 21:1—22:12
51	☐ 23:1—24:27	☐ 25:1—26:23	☐ 27:1—28:27	☐ 29:1-36	☐ 30:1—31:21	☐ 32:1-33	☐ 33:1—34:33
52	☐ 35:1—36:23	☐ Ezra 1:1-11	☐ 2:1-70	☐ 3:1—4:24	☐ 5:1—6:22	☐ 7:1-28	☐ 8:1-36

Reading Schedule for the Recovery Version of the Old Testament with Footnotes

Wk.	Lord's Day	Monday	Tuesday	Wednesday	Thursday	Friday	Saturday
53	☐ 9:1—10:44	☐ Neh 1:1-11	☐ 2:1—3:32	☐ 4:1—5:19	☐ 6:1-19	☐ 7:1-73	☐ 8:1-18
54	☐ 9:1-20	☐ 9:21-38	☐ 10:1—11:36	☐ 12:1-47	☐ 13:1-31	☐ Esth 1:1-22	☐ 2:1—3:15
55	☐ 4:1—5:14	☐ 6:1—7:10	☐ 8:1-17	☐ 9:1—10:3	☐ Job 1:1-22	☐ 2:1—3:26	☐ 4:1—5:27
56	☐ 6:1—7:21	☐ 8:1—9:35	☐ 10:1—11:20	☐ 12:1—13:28	☐ 14:1—15:35	☐ 16:1—17:16	☐ 18:1—19:29
57	☐ 20:1—21:34	☐ 22:1—23:17	☐ 24:1—25:6	☐ 26:1—27:23	☐ 28:1—29:25	☐ 30:1—31:40	☐ 32:1—33:33
58	☐ 34:1—35:16	☐ 36:1-33	☐ 37:1-24	☐ 38:1-41	☐ 39:1-30	☐ 40:1-24	☐ 41:1-34
59	☐ 42:1-17	☐ Psa 1:1-6	☐ 2:1—3:8	☐ 4:1—6:10	☐ 7:1—8:9	☐ 9:1—10:18	☐ 11:1—15:5
60	☐ 16:1—17:15	☐ 18:1-50	☐ 19:1—21:13	☐ 22:1-31	☐ 23:1—24:10	☐ 25:1—27:14	☐ 28:1—30:12
61	☐ 31:1—32:11	☐ 33:1—34:22	☐ 35:1—36:12	☐ 37:1-40	☐ 38:1—39:13	☐ 40:1—41:13	☐ 42:1—43:5
62	☐ 44:1-26	☐ 45:1-17	☐ 46:1—48:14	☐ 49:1—50:23	☐ 51:1—52:9	☐ 53:1—55:23	☐ 56:1—58:11
63	☐ 59:1—61:8	☐ 62:1—64:10	☐ 65:1—67:7	☐ 68:1-35	☐ 69:1—70:5	☐ 71:1—72:20	☐ 73:1—74:23
64	☐ 75:1—77:20	☐ 78:1-72	☐ 79:1—81:16	☐ 82:1—84:12	☐ 85:1—87:7	☐ 88:1—89:52	☐ 90:1—91:16
65	☐ 92:1—94:23	☐ 95:1—97:12	☐ 98:1—101:8	☐ 102:1—103:22	☐ 104:1—105:45	☐ 106:1-48	☐ 107:1-43
66	☐ 108:1—109:31	☐ 110:1—112:10	☐ 113:1—115:18	☐ 116:1—118:29	☐ 119:1-32	☐ 119:33-72	☐ 119:73-120
67	☐ 119:121-176	☐ 120:1—124:8	☐ 125:1—128:6	☐ 129:1—132:18	☐ 133:1—135:21	☐ 136:1—138:8	☐ 139:1—140:13
68	☐ 141:1—144:15	☐ 145:1—147:20	☐ 148:1—150:6	☐ Prov 1:1-33	☐ 2:1—3:35	☐ 4:1—5:23	☐ 6:1-35
69	☐ 7:1—8:36	☐ 9:1—10:32	☐ 11:1—12:28	☐ 13:1—14:35	☐ 15:1-33	☐ 16:1-33	☐ 17:1-28
70	☐ 18:1-24	☐ 19:1—20:30	☐ 21:1—22:29	☐ 23:1-35	☐ 24:1—25:28	☐ 26:1—27:27	☐ 28:1—29:27
71	☐ 30:1-33	☐ 31:1-31	☐ Eccl 1:1-18	☐ 2:1—3:22	☐ 4:1—5:20	☐ 6:1—7:29	☐ 8:1—9:18
72	☐ 10:1—11:10	☐ 12:1-14	☐ S.S 1:1-8	☐ 1:9-17	☐ 2:1-17	☐ 3:1-11	☐ 4:1-8
73	☐ 4:9-16	☐ 5:1-16	☐ 6:1-13	☐ 7:1-13	☐ 8:1-14	☐ Isa 1:1-11	☐ 1:12-31
74	☐ 2:1-22	☐ 3:1-26	☐ 4:1-6	☐ 5:1-30	☐ 6:1-13	☐ 7:1-25	☐ 8:1-22
75	☐ 9:1-21	☐ 10:1-34	☐ 11:1—12:6	☐ 13:1-22	☐ 14:1-14	☐ 14:15-32	☐ 15:1—16:14
76	☐ 17:1—18:7	☐ 19:1-25	☐ 20:1—21:17	☐ 22:1-25	☐ 23:1-18	☐ 24:1-23	☐ 25:1-12
77	☐ 26:1-21	☐ 27:1-13	☐ 28:1-29	☐ 29:1-24	☐ 30:1-33	☐ 31:1—32:20	☐ 33:1-24
78	☐ 34:1-17	☐ 35:1-10	☐ 36:1-22	☐ 37:1-38	☐ 38:1—39:8	☐ 40:1-31	☐ 41:1-29

Reading Schedule for the Recovery Version of the Old Testament with Footnotes

Wk.	Lord's Day	Monday	Tuesday	Wednesday	Thursday	Friday	Saturday
79	☐ 42:1-25	☐ 43:1-28	☐ 44:1-28	☐ 45:1-25	☐ 46:1-13	☐ 47:1-15	☐ 48:1-22
80	☐ 49:1-13	☐ 49:14-26	☐ 50:1—51:23	☐ 52:1-15	☐ 53:1-12	☐ 54:1-17	☐ 55:1-13
81	☐ 56:1-12	☐ 57:1-21	☐ 58:1-14	☐ 59:1-21	☐ 60:1-22	☐ 61:1-11	☐ 62:1-12
82	☐ 63:1-19	☐ 64:1-12	☐ 65:1-25	☐ 66:1-24	☐ Jer 1:1-19	☐ 2:1-19	☐ 2:20-37
83	☐ 3:1-25	☐ 4:1-31	☐ 5:1-31	☐ 6:1-30	☐ 7:1-34	☐ 8:1-22	☐ 9:1-26
84	☐ 10:1-25	☐ 11:1—12:17	☐ 13:1-27	☐ 14:1-22	☐ 15:1-21	☐ 16:1—17:27	☐ 18:1-23
85	☐ 19:1—20:18	☐ 21:1—22:30	☐ 23:1-40	☐ 24:1—25:38	☐ 26:1—27:22	☐ 28:1—29:32	☐ 30:1-24
86	☐ 31:1-23	☐ 31:24-40	☐ 32:1-44	☐ 33:1-26	☐ 34:1-22	☐ 35:1-19	☐ 36:1-32
87	☐ 37:1-21	☐ 38:1-28	☐ 39:1—40:16	☐ 41:1—42:22	☐ 43:1—44:30	☐ 45:1—46:28	☐ 47:1—48:16
88	☐ 48:17-47	☐ 49:1-22	☐ 49:23-39	☐ 50:1-27	☐ 50:28-46	☐ 51:1-27	☐ 51:28-64
89	☐ 52:1-34	☐ Lam 1:1-22	☐ 2:1-22	☐ 3:1-39	☐ 3:40-66	☐ 4:1-22	☐ 5:1-22
90	☐ Ezek 1:1-14	☐ 1:15-28	☐ 2:1—3:27	☐ 4:1—5:17	☐ 6:1—7:27	☐ 8:1—9:11	☐ 10:1—11:25
91	☐ 12:1—13:23	☐ 14:1—15:8	☐ 16:1-63	☐ 17:1—18:32	☐ 19:1-14	☐ 20:1-49	☐ 21:1-32
92	☐ 22:1-31	☐ 23:1-49	☐ 24:1-27	☐ 25:1—26:21	☐ 27:1-36	☐ 28:1-26	☐ 29:1—30:26
93	☐ 31:1—32:32	☐ 33:1-33	☐ 34:1-31	☐ 35:1—36:21	☐ 36:22-38	☐ 37:1-28	☐ 38:1—39:29
94	☐ 40:1-27	☐ 40:28-49	☐ 41:1-26	☐ 42:1—43:27	☐ 44:1-31	☐ 45:1-25	☐ 46:1-24
95	☐ 47:1-23	☐ 48:1-35	☐ Dan 1:1-21	☐ 2:1-30	☐ 2:31-49	☐ 3:1-30	☐ 4:1-37
96	☐ 5:1-31	☐ 6:1-28	☐ 7:1-12	☐ 7:13-28	☐ 8:1-27	☐ 9:1-27	☐ 10:1-21
97	☐ 11:1-22	☐ 11:23-45	☐ 12:1-13	☐ Hosea 1:1-11	☐ 2:1-23	☐ 3:1—4:19	☐ 5:1-15
98	☐ 6:1-11	☐ 7:1-16	☐ 8:1-14	☐ 9:1-17	☐ 10:1-15	☐ 11:1-12	☐ 12:1-14
99	☐ 13:1—14:9	☐ Joel 1:1-20	☐ 2:1-16	☐ 2:17-32	☐ 3:1-21	☐ Amos 1:1-15	☐ 2:1-16
100	☐ 3:1-15	☐ 4:1—5:27	☐ 6:1—7:17	☐ 8:1—9:15	☐ Obad 1-21	☐ Jonah 1:1-17	☐ 2:1—4:11
101	☐ Micah 1:1-16	☐ 2:1—3:12	☐ 4:1—5:15	☐ 6:1—7:20	☐ Nahum 1:1-15	☐ 2:1—3:19	☐ Hab 1:1-17
102	☐ 2:1-20	☐ 3:1-19	☐ Zeph 1:1-18	☐ 2:1-15	☐ 3:1-20	☐ Hag 1:1-15	☐ 2:1-23
103	☐ Zech 1:1-21	☐ 2:1-13	☐ 3:1-10	☐ 4:1-14	☐ 5:1—6:15	☐ 7:1—8:23	☐ 9:1-17
104	☐ 10:1—11:17	☐ 12:1—13:9	☐ 14:1-21	☐ Mal 1:1-14	☐ 2:1-17	☐ 3:1-18	☐ 4:1-6

Reading Schedule for the Recovery Version of the New Testament with Footnotes

Wk.	Lord's Day	Monday	Tuesday	Wednesday	Thursday	Friday	Saturday
1	☐ Matt 1:1-2	☐ 1:3-7	☐ 1:8-17	☐ 1:18-25	☐ 2:1-23	☐ 3:1-6	☐ 3:7-17
2	☐ 4:1-11	☐ 4:12-25	☐ 5:1-4	☐ 5:5-12	☐ 5:13-20	☐ 5:21-26	☐ 5:27-48
3	☐ 6:1-8	☐ 6:9-18	☐ 6:19-34	☐ 7:1-12	☐ 7:13-29	☐ 8:1-13	☐ 8:14-22
4	☐ 8:23-34	☐ 9:1-13	☐ 9:14-17	☐ 9:18-34	☐ 9:35—10:5	☐ 10:6-25	☐ 10:26-42
5	☐ 11:1-15	☐ 11:16-30	☐ 12:1-14	☐ 12:15-32	☐ 12:33-42	☐ 12:43—13:2	☐ 13:3-12
6	☐ 13:13-30	☐ 13:31-43	☐ 13:44-58	☐ 14:1-13	☐ 14:14-21	☐ 14:22-36	☐ 15:1-20
7	☐ 15:21-31	☐ 15:32-39	☐ 16:1-12	☐ 16:13-20	☐ 16:21-28	☐ 17:1-13	☐ 17:14-27
8	☐ 18:1-14	☐ 18:15-22	☐ 18:23-35	☐ 19:1-15	☐ 19:16-30	☐ 20:1-16	☐ 20:17-34
9	☐ 21:1-11	☐ 21:12-22	☐ 21:23-32	☐ 21:33-46	☐ 22:1-22	☐ 22:23-33	☐ 22:34-46
10	☐ 23:1-12	☐ 23:13-39	☐ 24:1-14	☐ 24:15-31	☐ 24:32-51	☐ 25:1-13	☐ 25:14-30
11	☐ 25:31-46	☐ 26:1-16	☐ 26:17-35	☐ 26:36-46	☐ 26:47-64	☐ 26:65-75	☐ 27:1-26
12	☐ 27:27-44	☐ 27:45-56	☐ 27:57—28:15	☐ 28:16-20	☐ Mark 1:1	☐ 1:2-6	☐ 1:7-13
13	☐ 1:14-28	☐ 1:29-45	☐ 2:1-12	☐ 2:13-28	☐ 3:1-19	☐ 3:20-35	☐ 4:1-25
14	☐ 4:26-41	☐ 5:1-20	☐ 5:21-43	☐ 6:1-29	☐ 6:30-56	☐ 7:1-23	☐ 7:24-37
15	☐ 8:1-26	☐ 8:27—9:1	☐ 9:2-29	☐ 9:30-50	☐ 10:1-16	☐ 10:17-34	☐ 10:35-52
16	☐ 11:1-16	☐ 11:17-33	☐ 12:1-27	☐ 12:28-44	☐ 13:1-13	☐ 13:14-37	☐ 14:1-26
17	☐ 14:27-52	☐ 14:53-72	☐ 15:1-15	☐ 15:16-47	☐ 16:1-8	☐ 16:9-20	☐ Luke 1:1-4
18	☐ 1:5-25	☐ 1:26-46	☐ 1:47-56	☐ 1:57-80	☐ 2:1-8	☐ 2:9-20	☐ 2:21-39
19	☐ 2:40-52	☐ 3:1-20	☐ 3:21-38	☐ 4:1-13	☐ 4:14-30	☐ 4:31-44	☐ 5:1-26
20	☐ 5:27—6:16	☐ 6:17-38	☐ 6:39-49	☐ 7:1-17	☐ 7:18-23	☐ 7:24-35	☐ 7:36-50
21	☐ 8:1-15	☐ 8:16-25	☐ 8:26-39	☐ 8:40-56	☐ 9:1-17	☐ 9:18-26	☐ 9:27-36
22	☐ 9:37-50	☐ 9:51-62	☐ 10:1-11	☐ 10:12-24	☐ 10:25-37	☐ 10:38-42	☐ 11:1-13
23	☐ 11:14-26	☐ 11:27-36	☐ 11:37-54	☐ 12:1-12	☐ 12:13-21	☐ 12:22-34	☐ 12:35-48
24	☐ 12:49-59	☐ 13:1-9	☐ 13:10-17	☐ 13:18-30	☐ 13:31—14:6	☐ 14:7-14	☐ 14:15-24
25	☐ 14:25-35	☐ 15:1-10	☐ 15:11-21	☐ 15:22-32	☐ 16:1-13	☐ 16:14-22	☐ 16:23-31
26	☐ 17:1-19	☐ 17:20-37	☐ 18:1-14	☐ 18:15-30	☐ 18:31-43	☐ 19:1-10	☐ 19:11-27

Reading Schedule for the Recovery Version of the New Testament with Footnotes

Wk.	Lord's Day	Monday	Tuesday	Wednesday	Thursday	Friday	Saturday
27	☐ Luke 19:28-48	☐ 20:1-19	☐ 20:20-38	☐ 20:39—21:4	☐ 21:5-27	☐ 21:28-38	☐ 22:1-20
28	☐ 22:21-38	☐ 22:39-54	☐ 22:55-71	☐ 23:1-43	☐ 23:44-56	☐ 24:1-12	☐ 24:13-35
29	☐ 24:36-53	☐ John 1:1-13	☐ 1:14-18	☐ 1:19-34	☐ 1:35-51	☐ 2:1-11	☐ 2:12-22
30	☐ 2:23—3:13	☐ 3:14-21	☐ 3:22-36	☐ 4:1-14	☐ 4:15-26	☐ 4:27-42	☐ 4:43-54
31	☐ 5:1-16	☐ 5:17-30	☐ 5:31-47	☐ 6:1-15	☐ 6:16-31	☐ 6:32-51	☐ 6:52-71
32	☐ 7:1-9	☐ 7:10-24	☐ 7:25-36	☐ 7:37-52	☐ 7:53—8:11	☐ 8:12-27	☐ 8:28-44
33	☐ 8:45-59	☐ 9:1-13	☐ 9:14-34	☐ 9:35—10:9	☐ 10:10-30	☐ 10:31—11:4	☐ 11:5-22
34	☐ 11:23-40	☐ 11:41-57	☐ 12:1-11	☐ 12:12-24	☐ 12:25-36	☐ 12:37-50	☐ 13:1-11
35	☐ 13:12-30	☐ 13:31-38	☐ 14:1-6	☐ 14:7-20	☐ 14:21-31	☐ 15:1-11	☐ 15:12-27
36	☐ 16:1-15	☐ 16:16-33	☐ 17:1-5	☐ 17:6-13	☐ 17:14-24	☐ 17:25—18:11	☐ 18:12-27
37	☐ 18:28-40	☐ 19:1-16	☐ 19:17-30	☐ 19:31-42	☐ 20:1-13	☐ 20:14-18	☐ 20:19-22
38	☐ 20:23-31	☐ 21:1-14	☐ 21:15-22	☐ 21:23-25	☐ Acts 1:1-8	☐ 1:9-14	☐ 1:15-26
39	☐ 2:1-13	☐ 2:14-21	☐ 2:22-36	☐ 2:37-41	☐ 2:42-47	☐ 3:1-18	☐ 3:19—4:22
40	☐ 4:23-37	☐ 5:1-16	☐ 5:17-32	☐ 5:33-42	☐ 6:1—7:1	☐ 7:2-29	☐ 7:30-60
41	☐ 8:1-13	☐ 8:14-25	☐ 8:26-40	☐ 9:1-19	☐ 9:20-43	☐ 10:1-16	☐ 10:17-33
42	☐ 10:34-48	☐ 11:1-18	☐ 11:19-30	☐ 12:1-25	☐ 13:1-12	☐ 13:13-43	☐ 13:44—14:5
43	☐ 14:6-28	☐ 15:1-12	☐ 15:13-34	☐ 15:35—16:5	☐ 16:6-18	☐ 16:19-40	☐ 17:1-18
44	☐ 17:19-34	☐ 18:1-17	☐ 18:18-28	☐ 19:1-20	☐ 19:21-41	☐ 20:1-12	☐ 20:13-38
45	☐ 21:1-14	☐ 21:15-26	☐ 21:27-40	☐ 22:1-21	☐ 22:22-29	☐ 22:30—23:11	☐ 23:12-15
46	☐ 23:16-30	☐ 23:31—24:21	☐ 24:22—25:5	☐ 25:6-27	☐ 26:1-13	☐ 26:14-32	☐ 27:1-26
47	☐ 27:27—28:10	☐ 28:11-22	☐ 28:23-31	☐ Rom 1:1-2	☐ 1:3-7	☐ 1:8-17	☐ 1:18-25
48	☐ 1:26—2:10	☐ 2:11-29	☐ 3:1-20	☐ 3:21-31	☐ 4:1-12	☐ 4:13-25	☐ 5:1-11
49	☐ 5:12-17	☐ 5:18—6:5	☐ 6:6-11	☐ 6:12-23	☐ 7:1-12	☐ 7:13-25	☐ 8:1-2
50	☐ 8:3-6	☐ 8:7-13	☐ 8:14-25	☐ 8:26-39	☐ 9:1-18	☐ 9:19—10:3	☐ 10:4-15
51	☐ 10:16—11:10	☐ 11:11-22	☐ 11:23-36	☐ 12:1-3	☐ 12:4-21	☐ 13:1-14	☐ 14:1-12
52	☐ 14:13-23	☐ 15:1-13	☐ 15:14-33	☐ 16:1-5	☐ 16:6-24	☐ 16:25-27	☐ 1 Cor 1:1-4

Reading Schedule for the Recovery Version of the New Testament with Footnotes

Wk.	Lord's Day	Monday	Tuesday	Wednesday	Thursday	Friday	Saturday
53	☐ 1 Cor 1:5-9	☐ 1:10-17	☐ 1:18-31	☐ 2:1-5	☐ 2:6-10	☐ 2:11-16	☐ 3:1-9
54	☐ 3:10-13	☐ 3:14-23	☐ 4:1-9	☐ 4:10-21	☐ 5:1-13	☐ 6:1-11	☐ 6:12-20
55	☐ 7:1-16	☐ 7:17-24	☐ 7:25-40	☐ 8:1-13	☐ 9:1-15	☐ 9:16-27	☐ 10:1-4
56	☐ 10:5-13	☐ 10:14-33	☐ 11:1-6	☐ 11:7-16	☐ 11:17-26	☐ 11:27-34	☐ 12:1-11
57	☐ 12:12-22	☐ 12:23-31	☐ 13:1-13	☐ 14:1-12	☐ 14:13-25	☐ 14:26-33	☐ 14:34-40
58	☐ 15:1-19	☐ 15:20-28	☐ 15:29-34	☐ 15:35-49	☐ 15:50-58	☐ 16:1-9	☐ 16:10-24
59	☐ 2 Cor 1:1-4	☐ 1:5-14	☐ 1:15-22	☐ 1:23—2:11	☐ 2:12-17	☐ 3:1-6	☐ 3:7-11
60	☐ 3:12-18	☐ 4:1-6	☐ 4:7-12	☐ 4:13-18	☐ 5:1-8	☐ 5:9-15	☐ 5:16-21
61	☐ 6:1-13	☐ 6:14—7:4	☐ 7:5-16	☐ 8:1-15	☐ 8:16-24	☐ 9:1-15	☐ 10:1-6
62	☐ 10:7-18	☐ 11:1-15	☐ 11:16-33	☐ 12:1-10	☐ 12:11-21	☐ 13:1-10	☐ 13:11-14
63	☐ Gal 1:1-5	☐ 1:6-14	☐ 1:15-24	☐ 2:1-13	☐ 2:14-21	☐ 3:1-4	☐ 3:5-14
64	☐ 3:15-22	☐ 3:23-29	☐ 4:1-7	☐ 4:8-20	☐ 4:21-31	☐ 5:1-12	☐ 5:13-21
65	☐ 5:22-26	☐ 6:1-10	☐ 6:11-15	☐ 6:16-18	☐ Eph 1:1-3	☐ 1:4-6	☐ 1:7-10
66	☐ 1:11-14	☐ 1:15-18	☐ 1:19-23	☐ 2:1-5	☐ 2:6-10	☐ 2:11-14	☐ 2:15-18
67	☐ 2:19-22	☐ 3:1-7	☐ 3:8-13	☐ 3:14-18	☐ 3:19-21	☐ 4:1-4	☐ 4:5-10
68	☐ 4:11-16	☐ 4:17-24	☐ 4:25-32	☐ 5:1-10	☐ 5:11-21	☐ 5:22-26	☐ 5:27-33
69	☐ 6:1-9	☐ 6:10-14	☐ 6:15-18	☐ 6:19-24	☐ Phil 1:1-7	☐ 1:8-18	☐ 1:19-26
70	☐ 1:27—2:4	☐ 2:5-11	☐ 2:12-16	☐ 2:17-30	☐ 3:1-6`	☐ 3:7-11	☐ 3:12-16
71	☐ 3:17-21	☐ 4:1-9	☐ 4:10-23	☐ Col 1:1-8	☐ 1:9-13	☐ 1:14-23	☐ 1:24-29
72	☐ 2:1-7	☐ 2:8-15	☐ 2:16-23	☐ 3:1-4	☐ 3:5-15	☐ 3:16-25	☐ 4:1-18
73	☐ 1 Thes 1:1-3	☐ 1:4-10	☐ 2:1-12	☐ 2:13—3:5	☐ 3:6-13	☐ 4:1-10	☐ 4:11—5:11
74	☐ 5:12-28	☐ 2 Thes 1:1-12	☐ 2:1-17	☐ 3:1-18	☐ 1 Tim 1:1-2	☐ 1:3-4	☐ 1:5-14
75	☐ 1:15-20	☐ 2:1-7	☐ 2:8-15	☐ 3:1-13	☐ 3:14—4:5	☐ 4:6-16	☐ 5:1-25
76	☐ 6:1-10	☐ 6:11-21	☐ 2 Tim 1:1-10	☐ 1:11-18	☐ 2:1-15	☐ 2:16-26	☐ 3:1-13
77	☐ 3:14—4:8	☐ 4:9-22	☐ Titus 1:1-4	☐ 1:5-16	☐ 2:1-15	☐ 3:1-8	☐ 3:9-15
78	☐ Philem 1:1-11	☐ 1:12-25	☐ Heb 1:1-2	☐ 1:3-5	☐ 1:6-14	☐ 2:1-9	☐ 2:10-18

Reading Schedule for the Recovery Version of the New Testament with Footnotes

Wk.	Lord's Day	Monday	Tuesday	Wednesday	Thursday	Friday	Saturday
79	☐ Heb 3:1-6	☐ 3:7-19	☐ 4:1-9	☐ 4:10-13	☐ 4:14-16	☐ 5:1-10	☐ 5:11—6:3
80	☐ 6:4-8	☐ 6:9-20	☐ 7:1-10	☐ 7:11-28	☐ 8:1-6	☐ 8:7-13	☐ 9:1-4
81	☐ 9:5-14	☐ 9:15-28	☐ 10:1-18	☐ 10:19-28	☐ 10:29-39	☐ 11:1-6	☐ 11:7-19
82	☐ 11:20-31	☐ 11:32-40	☐ 12:1-2	☐ 12:3-13	☐ 12:14-17	☐ 12:18-26	☐ 12:27-29
83	☐ 13:1-7	☐ 13:8-12	☐ 13:13-15	☐ 13:16-25	☐ James 1:1-8	☐ 1:9-18	☐ 1:19-27
84	☐ 2:1-13	☐ 2:14-26	☐ 3:1-18	☐ 4:1-10	☐ 4:11-17	☐ 5:1-12	☐ 5:13-20
85	☐ 1 Pet 1:1-2	☐ 1:3-4	☐ 1:5	☐ 1:6-9	☐ 1:10-12	☐ 1:13-17	☐ 1:18-25
86	☐ 2:1-3	☐ 2:4-8	☐ 2:9-17	☐ 2:18-25	☐ 3:1-13	☐ 3:14-22	☐ 4:1-6
87	☐ 4:7-16	☐ 4:17-19	☐ 5:1-4	☐ 5:5-9	☐ 5:10-14	☐ 2 Pet 1:1-2	☐ 1:3-4
88	☐ 1:5-8	☐ 1:9-11	☐ 1:12-18	☐ 1:19-21	☐ 2:1-3	☐ 2:4-11	☐ 2:12-22
89	☐ 3:1-6	☐ 3:7-9	☐ 3:10-12	☐ 3:13-15	☐ 3:16	☐ 3:17-18	☐ 1 John 1:1-2
90	☐ 1:3-4	☐ 1:5	☐ 1:6	☐ 1:7	☐ 1:8-10	☐ 2:1-2	☐ 2:3-11
91	☐ 2:12-14	☐ 2:15-19	☐ 2:20-23	☐ 2:24-27	☐ 2:28-29	☐ 3:1-5	☐ 3:6-10
92	☐ 3:11-18	☐ 3:19-24	☐ 4:1-6	☐ 4:7-11	☐ 4:12-15	☐ 4:16—5:3	☐ 5:4-13
93	☐ 5:14-17	☐ 5:18-21	☐ 2 John 1:1-3	☐ 1:4-9	☐ 1:10-13	☐ 3 John 1:1-6	☐ 1:7-14
94	☐ Jude 1:1-4	☐ 1:5-10	☐ 1:11-19	☐ 1:20-25	☐ Rev 1:1-3	☐ 1:4-6	☐ 1:7-11
95	☐ 1:12-13	☐ 1:14-16	☐ 1:17-20	☐ 2:1-6	☐ 2:7	☐ 2:8-9	☐ 2:10-11
96	☐ 2:12-14	☐ 2:15-17	☐ 2:18-23	☐ 2:24-29	☐ 3:1-3	☐ 3:4-6	☐ 3:7-9
97	☐ 3:10-13	☐ 3:14-18	☐ 3:19-22	☐ 4:1-5	☐ 4:6-7	☐ 4:8-11	☐ 5:1-6
98	☐ 5:7-14	☐ 6:1-8	☐ 6:9-17	☐ 7:1-8	☐ 7:9-17	☐ 8:1-6	☐ 8:7-12
99	☐ 8:13—9:11	☐ 9:12-21	☐ 10:1-4	☐ 10:5-11	☐ 11:1-4	☐ 11:5-14	☐ 11:15-19
100	☐ 12:1-4	☐ 12:5-9	☐ 12:10-18	☐ 13:1-10	☐ 13:11-18	☐ 14:1-5	☐ 14:6-12
101	☐ 14:13-20	☐ 15:1-8	☐ 16:1-12	☐ 16:13-21	☐ 17:1-6	☐ 17:7-18	☐ 18:1-8
102	☐ 18:9—19:4	☐ 19:5-10	☐ 19:11-16	☐ 19:17-21	☐ 20:1-6	☐ 20:7-10	☐ 20:11-15
103	☐ 21:1	☐ 21:2	☐ 21:3-8	☐ 21:9-13	☐ 21:14-18	☐ 21:19-21	☐ 21:22-27
104	☐ 22:1	☐ 22:2	☐ 22:3-11	☐ 22:12-15	☐ 22:16-17	☐ 22:18-21	

Week 1 — Day 6   Today's verses

1 Tim. Holding the mystery of the faith in a pure
3:9   conscience.
15 But if I delay, *I write* that you may know how one ought to conduct himself in the house of God, which is the church of the living God, the pillar and base of the truth.

Week 1 — Day 5   Today's verses

2 Pet. Through which He has granted to us pre-
1:4   cious and exceedingly great promises that through these you might become partakers of the divine nature...

Col. For in Him dwells all the fullness of the
2:9   Godhead bodily.

Rev. ...*There were* seven lamps of fire burning
4:5   before the throne, which are the seven Spirits of God.

Date

Week 1 — Day 4   Today's verses

Rev. Who testified the word of God and the
1:2   testimony of Jesus Christ, *even* all that he saw.
9 I John, your brother and fellow partaker in the tribulation and kingdom and endurance in Jesus, was on the island called Patmos because of the word of God and the testimony of Jesus.

Date

Week 1 — Day 3   Today's verses

Rev. Saying, What you see write in a scroll
1:11   and send *it* to the seven churches...
12 And I turned to see the voice that spoke with me; and when I turned, I saw seven golden lampstands.
20 The mystery of the seven stars which you saw upon My right hand and the seven golden lampstands: The seven stars are the messengers of the seven churches, and the seven lampstands are the seven churches.

Date

Week 1 — Day 2   Today's verses

Eph. That He would grant you, according to
3:16-17   the riches of His glory, to be strengthened with power through His Spirit into the inner man, that Christ may make His home in your hearts through faith...
19 ...That you may be filled unto all the fullness of God.

Date

Week 1 — Day 1   Today's verses

Prov. Where there is no vision, the people cast
29:18   off restraint...

Acts Therefore, King Agrippa, I was not dis-
26:19   obedient to the heavenly vision.

Eph. One Body and one Spirit, even as also
4:4-6   you were called in one hope of your calling; one Lord, one faith, one baptism; one God and Father of all, who is over all and through all and in all.

Date

Week 2 — Day 4   Today's verses

Matt. 28:19   Go therefore and disciple all the nations, baptizing them into the name of the Father and of the Son and of the Holy Spirit.

2 Cor. 13:14   The grace of the Lord Jesus Christ and the love of God and the fellowship of the Holy Spirit be with you all.

Date

Week 2 — Day 5   Today's verses

Eph. 5:18-20   And do not be drunk with wine, in which is dissoluteness, but be filled in spirit, speaking to one another in psalms and hymns and spiritual songs,…giving thanks at all times for all things in the name of our Lord Jesus Christ to our God and Father.

Date

Week 2 — Day 6   Today's verses

Eph. 4:15-16   But holding to truth in love, we may grow up into Him in all things, who is the Head, Christ, out from whom all the Body, being joined together and being knit together through every joint of the rich supply and *through* the operation in the measure of each one part, causes the growth of the Body unto the building up of itself in love.

Date

Week 2 — Day 1   Today's verses

Rom. 5:5-6   …The love of God has been poured out in our hearts through the Holy Spirit, who has been given to us. For while we were yet weak, in due time Christ died for the ungodly.

8:9   But you are not in the flesh, but in the spirit, if indeed the Spirit of God dwells in you. Yet if anyone does not have the Spirit of Christ, he is not of Him.

Date

Week 2 — Day 2   Today's verses

Eph. 3:16-17   That He would grant you, according to the riches of His glory, to be strengthened with power through His Spirit into the inner man, that Christ may make His home in your hearts through faith.…

Rom 8:11   …If the Spirit of the One who raised Jesus from the dead dwells in you, He who raised Christ from the dead will also give life to your mortal bodies through His Spirit who indwells you.

Date

Week 2 — Day 3   Today's verses

Rom. 15:16   That I might be a minister of Christ Jesus to the Gentiles, a laboring priest of the gospel of God, in order that the offering of the Gentiles might be acceptable, having been sanctified in the Holy Spirit.

1 Pet. 1:2   Chosen according to the foreknowledge of God the Father in the sanctification of the Spirit unto the obedience and sprinkling of the blood of Jesus Christ: Grace to you and peace be multiplied.

Date

Week 3 — Day 4   Today's verses

Rom. And we know that all things work together
8:28-30 for good to those who love God, to those
who are called according to *His* purpose.
Because those whom He foreknew, He also
predestinated *to be* conformed to the image
of His Son, that He might be the Firstborn
among many brothers; and those whom
He predestinated, these He also called; and
those whom He called, these He also justified; and those whom He justified, these He
also glorified.

Date

Week 3 — Day 5   Today's verses

Rom. 8:9 But you are not in the flesh, but in the
spirit, if indeed the Spirit of God dwells in
you. Yet if anyone does not have the Spirit
of Christ, he is not of Him.

11 And if the Spirit of the One who raised Jesus from the dead dwells in you, He who
raised Christ from the dead will also give
life to your mortal bodies through His
Spirit who indwells you.

Date

Week 3 — Day 6   Today's verses

Rom. If Christ is in you, though the body is
8:10 dead because of sin, the spirit is life because of righteousness.

6 ...The mind set on the spirit is life and
peace.

11 ...If the Spirit of the One who raised Jesus
from the dead dwells in you, He who
raised Christ from the dead will also give
life to your mortal bodies through His
Spirit who indwells you.

Date

Week 3 — Day 1   Today's verses

Rom. 8:2 For the law of the Spirit of life has freed me
in Christ Jesus from the law of sin and of
death.

10-11 But if Christ is in you, though the body is
dead because of sin, the spirit is life because
of righteousness. And if the Spirit of the One
who raised Jesus from the dead dwells in
you, He who raised Christ from the dead will
also give life to your mortal bodies through
His Spirit who indwells you.

Date

Week 3 — Day 2   Today's verses

Rom. That the righteous requirement of the law
8:4-6 might be fulfilled in us, who do not walk
according to the flesh but according to the
spirit. For those who are according to the
flesh mind the things of the flesh; but
those who are according to the spirit, the
things of the Spirit. For the mind set on the
flesh is death, but the mind set on the spirit
is life and peace.

Date

Week 3 — Day 3   Today's verses

Rom. For as many as are led by the Spirit of
8:14-15 God, these are sons of God. For you have
not received a spirit of slavery *bringing
you* into fear again, but you have received a spirit of sonship in which we
cry, Abba, Father!

Date

Week 4 — Day 4   Today's verses

2 Cor. And having the same spirit of faith accord-
4:13   ing to that which is written, "I believed,
       therefore I spoke," we also believe, there-
       fore we also speak.

John   I am the vine; you are the branches. He
15:5   who abides in Me and I in him, he bears
       much fruit; for apart from Me you can do
       nothing.

_____
Date

Week 4 — Day 5   Today's verses

Rom. 8:4 That the righteous requirement of the law
         might be fulfilled in us, who do not walk
         according to the flesh but according to
         the spirit.

1 Cor.   But of Him you are in Christ Jesus, who
1:30   became wisdom to us from God: both
         righteousness and sanctification and
         redemption.

_____
Date

Week 4 — Day 6   Today's verses

Eph.   May be full of strength to apprehend with
3:18-20 all the saints what the breadth and length
        and height and depth are and to know the
        knowledge-surpassing love of Christ, that
        you may be filled unto all the fullness of
        God. But to Him who is able to do super-
        abundantly above all that we ask or think,
        according to the power which operates in
        us.

_____
Date

Week 4 — Day 1   Today's verses

Rom.   The Spirit Himself witnesses with our
8:16   spirit that we are children of God.

1 Cor. But he who is joined to the Lord is one
6:17   spirit.

_____
Date

Week 4 — Day 2   Today's verses

John   In that day you will know that I am in My
14:20 Father, and you in Me, and I in you.

Phil. For I know that for me this will turn out to
1:19   salvation through your petition and the
       bountiful supply of the Spirit of Jesus
       Christ.

21   For to me, to live is Christ...

_____
Date

Week 4 — Day 3   Today's verses

Rom. 8:9 But you are not in the flesh, but in the
         spirit, if indeed the Spirit of God dwells in
         you. Yet if anyone does not have the
         Spirit of Christ, he is not of Him.

11   And if the Spirit of the One who raised Je-
         sus from the dead dwells in you, He who
         raised Christ from the dead will also give
         life to your mortal bodies through His
         Spirit who indwells you.

_____
Date

Week 5 — Day 4   Today's verses

2 Cor. But thanks be to God, who always leads us
2:14-16 in triumph in the Christ and manifests the
savor of the knowledge of Him through us
in every place. For we are a fragrance of
Christ to God in those who are being saved
and in those who are perishing: To some a
savor out of death unto death, and to the
others a savor out of life unto life....

Date

Week 5 — Day 5   Today's verses

2 Cor. You are our letter, inscribed in our hearts,
3:2-3 known and read by all men, since you are
being manifested that you are a letter of
Christ ministered by us, inscribed not with
ink but with the Spirit of the living God; not
in tablets of stone but in tablets of hearts of
flesh.

6 Who has also made us sufficient as ministers of a new covenant, *ministers* not of
the letter but of the Spirit; for the letter
kills, but the Spirit gives life.

Date

Week 5 — Day 6   Today's verses

2 Cor. But whenever *their heart* turns to the
3:16 Lord, the veil is taken away.
4:6-7 Because the God who said, Out of darkness light shall shine, is the One who
shined in our hearts to illuminate the
knowledge of the glory of God in the face
of Jesus Christ. But we have this treasure
in earthen vessels that the excellency of
the power may be of God and not out of
us.

Date

Week 5 — Day 1   Today's verses

2 Tim. And the things which you have heard
2:2 from me through many witnesses, these
commit to faithful men, who will be competent to teach others also.
1 Tim. If you lay these things before the brothers,
4:6 you will be a good minister of Christ Jesus,
being nourished with the words of the
faith and of the good teaching which you
have closely followed.

Date

Week 5 — Day 2   Today's verses

2 Tim. Suffer evil with *me* as a good soldier of
2:3-5 Christ Jesus. No one serving as a soldier entangles himself with the affairs of this life,
that he may please the one who enlisted
him. And also if anyone contends *in the
games*, he is not crowned unless he contends lawfully.
1 Cor. For also if the trumpet gives an uncertain
14:8 sound, who will prepare himself for battle?

Date

Week 5 — Day 3   Today's verses

2 Tim. The laboring farmer must be the first to
2:6 partake of the fruit.
15 Be diligent to present yourself approved
to God, an unashamed workman, cutting
straight the word of the truth.

Date